THE
MORAY
WAY
COMPANION

Norman Thomson has been charmed by the Moray countryside since boyhood. After some years teaching at Gordonstoun he moved to England but kept returning to Moray on holiday before making it his permanent home after his retirement. In 2009 he and Ann Dunn launched the concept of the Moray Way and later co-founded the increasingly popular Moray Walking Festival.

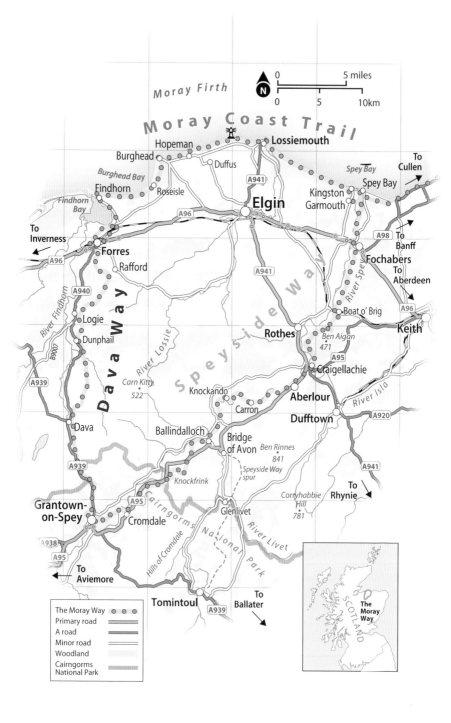

Moray Firth

0 5 miles

N

0   5   10km

Moray Coast Trail

Hopeman · · · · ☖ · · · · Lossiemouth

Burghead · · · · Duffus

Burghead Bay   A941

Findhorn · · · · Roseisle   *Spey Bay*   Spey Bay   To Cullen

Findhorn Bay   Kingston Garmouth

To Inverness   A96   Forres   A96   **Elgin**   A98 To Banff

Rafford   Fochabers   To Aberdeen

A940   A941   *River Spey*

D a v a   W a y   A96

Logie   Boat o' Brig   **Keith**

Dunphail   **Rothes**   *Ben Aigan* 471

B9007   *River Lossie*   **S p e y s i d e   W a y**   A95

Carn Kitty 522   Knockando   Craigellachie

A939   **Aberlour**   *River Isla*

Carron   **Dufftown**

Dava   Ballindalloch   Bridge of Avon   A920

A939   *Ben Rinnes* 841   A941

Knockfrink   *Speyside Way spur*   To Rhynie

Grantown-on-Spey   A95   **C a i r n g o r m s**   *Corryhabbie Hill* 781

Cromdale   Glenlivet   *River Livet*

A938   **N a t i o n a l   P a r k**

A95   *Hills of Cromdale*

To Aviemore   Tomintoul   A939   To Ballater

The Moray Way · · ·
Primary road
A road
Minor road
Woodland
Cairngorms National Park

SCOTLAND

The Moray Way

THE
MORAY
WAY
COMPANION

Norman Thomson

BIRLINN

First published in 2022 by Birlinn Ltd
West Newington House
10 Newington Road
Edinburgh
EH9 1QS

ISBN: 978 1 78027 793 6

Designed and typeset in Palatino
by Tom Johnstone Editorial Services

Printed and bound in Great Britain
by Bell & Bain Ltd, Glasgow

CONTENTS

MAPS

INTRODUCTION

There are many sites of historic, cultural and natural history interest conveniently close to the Moray Way. While some travellers may find that a hundred-mile path for walking fulfils all their exercise and adventure needs, many more are likely to combine their walking or cycling experience with breaks to explore interesting places or artefacts. The aim of this guide is to draw attention to the many such diversions that the Moray Way has to offer, and, for some readers at least, to point out opportunities which they might otherwise have missed which were close to their walks. No visitor will want to make *all* the diversions — if that were so, little time would be left for exploring the Moray Way itself! And of course for the determined walker for whom covering distance is all that counts, there will be only a few parts of the guide which are likely to be of interest. However surveys of participants in Moray Walking Festival events have shown that the guided walks which are most appreciated are those which feature information about, for example, history, wild life, geology, as well as drawing attention to museums and visitor centres.

With this in mind, sections 1 to 3 aim to point out things for a traveller to look out for *in geographical order* in the course of a clockwise journey round the Moray Way from Forres to Grantown via the Moray Coast Trail and the Speyside Way, and returning by the Dava Way. The lengths of these are about 32, 44 and 24 miles respectively, neatly totalling 100 miles. A condition for what is mentioned is that items included should be within one mile of the route. (There is one exception to this, namely at Craigellachie where diversions to Rothes and Dufftown

Opposite: Along the Moray Coast Trail.

deserve consideration.) There are points at which it would be over-prescriptive to give detailed step-by-step route descriptions. This is particularly true around the towns, where an entry point and an exit point for rejoining the Moray Way are sufficient information, leaving it to the visitor's discretion to select whatever features attract them most between the two.

It happens that most of Moray's many 'must see' points of interest lie within this one mile proximity, with two noteworthy ecclesiastical exceptions, namely the ruins of Elgin Cathedral and the Benedictine Abbey at Pluscarden, both of which are open all through the year and have their own handsomely produced guide books. Spynie Palace, a past stronghold of the warrior bishops of Moray which, like Elgin Cathedral, is now in the care of Historic Environment Scotland, is also worth seeing, as is another smaller building, namely the tiny Romanesque church at Birnie, seat of the first four twelfth and thirteenth-century bishops of Moray, which is still in regular use, and although normally locked, can be opened on request by phoning 01343 541328 or 07801 838947. Birnie Church lies close to the fields which were excavated in the 1990s and 2000s large Iron Age buildings were found, as well as the Birnie Hoard, a large collection of Roman coins, whose discovery caused considerable rethinking about the movements of the Romans in Britain. The Birnie Hoard is one of the highlights of the excellent Elgin Museum – another must see, but outside the immediate one mile range of the Moray Way. The museum, which is independent and run by volunteers, also contains a large collection of geological and fossil exhibits which demonstrate the long history of Moray over millennia. It also houses archaeological remains, notably those from Kineddar, just outside Lossiemouth, which was the religious centre of Moray prior to the commencement of the building of the cathedral in 1224.

'History' is a very broad term, and not everybody is likely to be interested in all aspects of what Moray has to offer. However the histories of whisky on the one hand,

and railways on the other, are likely to be of particular interest to quite a few walkers, as well as giving rise to many individual points of interest. Two sections therefore describe these sub-histories in chronological order, and this allows relatively short entries about whisky and railways to be included in the main narrative of sections 1 to 3 which guide a traveller making the clockwise circuit of the Moray Way starting at Forres.

Two human faculties underlie the fascination of history, namely imagination and discovery. The present did not come about by accident and there are many points on a circuit of the Moray Way where it is worthwhile to pause and consider imaginatively how the present evolved from the past. Hopefully this guide may trigger a few such moments by supplying some details of that past, while still leaving gaps open for further inspiration and discovery.

Incidentally, the Moray Way Association itself is not averse to making discoveries, so if you, the reader, find something you can tell us about or would like us to know, or possibly correct or update the information in this guide, please send an email to *ndt4@btinternet.com*.

Logos and Websites

The following logos will be encountered:

The Speyside Way logo.

Here are the websites for the routes:

www.morayways.org.uk/moray-coast-trail.asp
www.davaway.org.uk
www.speysideway.co.uk

Information about all three component routes is available on *www.scotlandsgreattrails.com*. Tidal information can be obtained by registering at *www.ukho.gov.uk/easytide*. Details of other historic paths can be found at *www.scotways.com* and *www.heritagepaths.co.uk*.

The Moray Way Association

The Moray Way was first conceived in 2009 when the idea of creating a circular long-distance trail comparable to Scotland's four official Long Distance Routes (the Speyside Way, the West Highland Way, the Southern Upland Way and the Great Glen Way) was first mooted.

Two well-attended public meetings in Elgin endorsed the idea, and the Moray Way Association was born, leading to the formation of a committee of volunteers to coordinate maintenance, improve way-finding, and encourage recreational use. A formal constitution was set out (the Association is now a registered charity, SC047381), and with generous help from Walkers of Aberlour the Moray Way map was published detailing the differing underfoot conditions on the various parts of the route. The map, costing £3.50 at the time of writing, is available at points along the route or by direct application to *ndt4@btinternet.com*. An updated version of this map appears in sections throughout this book. At a scale of 1:80,000, it is the first map at this sort of scale to cover all of Moray on a single sheet since the 1875 Ordnance Survey! Information about the Moray Way and indeed other footpaths in Moray can be found by visiting *www.morayways.org.uk*. This website is also the primary link for the annual Moray Walking Festival.

In 2011 the MWA committee realised that establishing a long-distance walking path was only a means to an end, and so decided to test the idea of organised walks along the route, the success of which led in 2012 to the first full-blown Moray Walking Festival, which has grown in numbers participating ever since – except for 2020!

Good signage has always been a core part of the Moray Way Association's endeavours, and if this has been successful few specific directional details should be needed in this guide. Consequently much of this text concerns places and features of interest along the route. Information about the paths connecting places and features is highlighted as green text in sections 1 to 3. For the towns, entry and exit signage points are readily found, thereby allowing the user flexibility of route choice within them.

The Moray Coast Trail

The full trail goes from Forres to Cullen and connects the intermediate villages and towns of Burghead, Hopeman, Lossiemouth, Garmouth, Kingston, Spey Bay, Port-gordon, Buckie, Portessie and Findochty (pronounced fin-ech-ty). It was first promoted in the early 2000s as a joint enterprise between Moray Council and local groups and interested parties. It was one of the original constitu-ents of the Scotland's Great Trails scheme launched by NatureScot (formerly Scottish Natural Heritage) in 2011.

The Speyside Way

The Speyside Way is one of four official Long Distance Routes in Scotland. It was first opened in 1981 from Spey Bay to Ballindalloch. A spur to Tomintoul (see p. 160) was added in 1990, followed by extensions to Buckie (1999) and Aviemore (2000). The route has now been formally completed to Newtonmore. The Speyside Way is man-aged by the three Access Authorities along the route – Moray Council, Highland Council and the Cairngorms National Park Authority.

The Dava Way

This component of the Moray Way is quite different in character from the other two. In 1996 a household survey on the development of Forres showed strong support for reopening the route of the abandoned railway line to Grantown-on-Spey as a walking and cycling path. This led to the foundation of the Dava Way Association as a not-for-profit company and registered charity (SC030496) with the initial aim of negotiating access, clearing the route, obtaining consultants' reports and raising funds. Eventually in 2002 the first diggers rolled in, and, with the crucial help of AJ Engineering Forres who gifted a metal bridge, the formal opening took place in 2005. Strong walkers can complete the route in a day; for cyclists four hours or so on a mountain bike is around the average time.

The processes of path maintenance and improvement are neverending, and increase all the time as the path's popularity increases. The Dava Way Association, which consists entirely of volunteers, works to make sure that the path surface is adequate to guarantee pleasant walking and cycling along its whole length. Periodic storms cause damage to the route through flooding, landslips and fallen trees, which at times can completely block the route. Rapid clearing together with improvements to drainage and path surfaces are costly, particularly where heavy machinery has to be hired. In May 2009 a BBC Breathing Place was opened at Edinkillie, partly funded by the Big Lottery Fund. This is now a popular entry point to the Dava Way, as well as a start point for a 1¼ mile/2km approach to the iconic Divie viaduct. In 2013 the Budge Foundation donated £20,000 for a project to enhance the route by further waymarking and interpretation aimed at preserving stories and folklore about the past inhabitants of the remoter parts of the moor. The results of this work are described in section 3. In 2009 a biennial overnight Ghost Train Walk from Grantown to Forres at midsummer was launched and has remained popular ever since.

The website *www.davaway.org.uk* is a source of up-to-date information on all aspects of the Dava Way.

The Dava Way is the major non-motor route through the thinly populated territory covered by the Finderne Community Council, which represents a region from Forres in the north to Dava in the south. Of the 24 miles of the Dava Way, 22 are in open country. Finderne Community Council is a voluntary organisation set up by statute to represent local residents and advise local government. Independent of this, Finderne Development Trust is a charity with ambitions for the area based on local consultation. Its logo will be observed on sign boards alongside that of the Dava Way.

Core Paths

A requirement of the Land Reform Act (Scotland) 2003 was that each Council produce a plan for a system of paths that provides a basic framework of routes sufficient for the purpose of giving the public a right of responsible, non-motorised access to most of the land and inland water of Scotland. A Core Path can physically be any route – a right of way, farm track, an old drove road, a minor public road or even a river. Moray's plan was produced in 2007/8 as a result of extensive public consultation. It was formally adopted in 2011. It deals with the area within the Council boundary, but does not include that part of Moray within the Cairngorms National Park, which has its own Core Paths plan, and is covered by a series of 39 highly detailed maps. All parts of the Moray Way, subject to this exclusion, are Core Paths. Queries about Core Paths can be addressed to *morayaccess@moray.gov.uk*.

Maps and Grid References

The Moray Way is covered by the following combinations of maps:

OS 1:50,000 Landranger: 27 Nairn & Forres; 28 Elgin & Dufftown; 36 Grantown & Cairngorm

OS 1:25,000 Explorer: 419 Grantown-on-Spey & Hills of Cromdale; 423 Elgin, Forres & Lossiemouth; 424 Buckie & Keith

The following maps each cover part of the Moray Way:

OS 1:25,000 Outdoor Leisure: OL61 Grantown-on-Spey & Hills of Cromdale

Harvey Maps: 1:40,000 Speyside Way, which includes the extension to Newtonmore

In some of the remoter areas, particularly in Section 4, grid references have been used to fix points whose locations are otherwise hard to describe.

Other Guide Books

The following guide books cover the Moray Way and the Speyside Way in varying levels of detail:

Sandra Bardwell, *Moray Coast Trail with Dava Way and Moray Way*, Rucksack Readers (second edition 2021).

Alan Castle, *The Speyside Way with the Dava Way and Moray Coast Trail*, Cicerone (2010, new edition 2016).

K. R. Fergus, *The Spey*, Pocket Mountains (2015). Covers some parts of the Speyside Way and has suggestions for other walks inspired by the Spey.

Jenny Main, *The Moray Coast*, Amberley Press (2011). For a wide variety of sites, this pairs old and current photographs on each page.

Jacquetta Megarry and Sandra Bardwell, *The Speyside Way*, Rucksack Readers (third edition 2021).

Geology

The main geology of the Moray Way is relatively straightforward. Moray is divided into approximately two contrasting halves as shown in the sketch below. Most of the Coastal trail overlies sandstones of the Devonian period of roughly 400 million years ago, except for a strip between Burghead and Hopeman which is younger, belonging to the Permian and early Jurassic periods of 200–250 million years ago (see p. 126). The Dava Way and Speyside Way cross areas of rock whose origins are meta-sediments from the period of the Dalriadan and Moinian supergroups dating from almost 1,000 million years ago, but heavily metamorphosed at the time of the Caledonian orogeny 465 million years ago. These are hard and partly quartzitic, as for example at Ben Aigan. Between Aberlour and Carron the path runs briefly over granite which is the western end of the Ben Rinnes complex. Ben Rinnes itself is the result of igneous intrusions, where hard rock did not succumb to glacial action. The average walker or cyclist is unlikely to be aware of these boundaries, but a few features are unmistakeable, such as the fault at Cove Bay near Hopeman, the foliation at Huntly's Cave on the Dava Way, the cliffs of unconsolidated glacially deposited material at the Dounie near Rothes, and of course the many caves, inlets and stacks between Burghead and Lossiemouth.

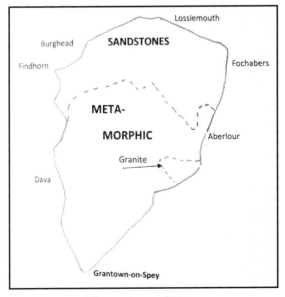

The geology of Moray.

Although the Moray coast has been rich in fossils, walkers on the Moray Way are unlikely to make any casual finds. However, Elgin Museum with its splendid local collections is an excellent place to reflect on the creatures which must have once inhabited this area, along with their environment.

Birds and Mammals

Moray is one of Britain's richest areas for birds, and some of the best spots to take advantage of this lie directly on the Moray Way, principally on the coastal trail section. Some spectacles are unmissable from any point, for example the skeins of wild geese in noisy V-formations arriving in late September/early October, and departing northwards in late March to breed in northern latitudes. Over 50,000 pink-footed geese spend the summer in Findhorn Bay, which, along with the Lossie estuary, are the best spots for 'interesting' sightings. The following list is a summary of some of the more distinctive birds which an observant, not necessarily expert visitor carrying binoculars might hope to see on the Moray Way, and to which references are made from time to time in the route descriptions. More serious birdwatching visitors should consult the superb website *www.birdsinmorayandnairn.org* on which enthusiasts and photographers report and display their most recent findings.

Spring: stonechat, greylag and pink-footed geese.

Summer: osprey, shelduck, terns (Arctic, Sandwich, common), wheatear.

Autumn and winter: wigeon, teal, turnstone, bar-tailed godwit, cormorant, scoter, red-breasted merganser, pintail, redshank, curlew, lapwing, snow bunting, dunlin, knot, long-tailed duck, whooper swans, red throated diver, gannet, purple sandpiper.

All year round: oystercatcher, eider, fulmar, yellowhammer, linnet, treecreeper.

Some of the above, such as golden plover and curlew, frequent the higher regions in the summer, then make their way to the coast in the latter part of the year. Summer visitors such as the chiffchaff and willow warblers are to be seen and heard in the birch woods, as are siskins which are partial migrants, and, in years when there is an irruption, Scottish crossbills.

Red squirrels are likely sightings in wooded areas, and increasingly so are pine martens. Stoats are seen occasionally, for example on the scrub land east of Findhorn. Mink are an unwelcome species and are still present on the Burghead–Hopeman stretch in spite of trapping. Otters are occasionally spotted, and bats of three British species – Pipistrelle, Daubentons and Long-eared – have been recorded.

Flowers

The flowers to be seen while you walk the Moray Way are so numerous, and so dependent on habitat and season, that it is only possible to mention here a few of the more exciting spectacles, namely the vivid yellows and fragrance of gorse in May and June particularly around Hopeman, the cascades of primroses in Primrose Bay to the east of Hopeman, the drifts of bog asphodel on Dava Moor in August, the acres of cotton grass in June, together with the more subtle abundance of gentians and marsh orchids north of Dava Station, and further north the bog-beans and marsh cinquefoil at Waypoint 10 (see p. 139).

The walker for whom floral discoveries are an important part of the experience does well to come equipped with one of the many available flower guides. At one end of the spectrum is the detailed and highly respected *The Wildflower Key* by Francis Rose and Clare O'Reilly (Warne, 2006). At the other is *Scottish Wild Flowers* by Michael Scott (Birlinn 2011) which not only fits into (largish) pockets, but arranges flowers conveniently by habitat, and references only those which might reasonably be found in Scotland. No longer in print, but a truly local and voluminous guide is *The Flora of Moray, Nairn and East Inverness* by Mary McCallum Webster (Aberdeen University Press, 1978).

Accommodation and Transport

Tourism is a major business in Moray and the area is well provided for with accommodation at every budget level. Changes are frequent and a good way to make enquiries is to visit *www.morayspeyside.com* and *www.greaterspeyside. com.*

Inverness is about 30 miles from the nearest point of the Moray Way, Aberdeen about 50. Both of these are well served by air, train and coach from many centres throughout the UK. There are passenger rail stations at Forres and Elgin. Suggested websites and phone numbers correct at time of writing are:

www.invernessairport.co.uk, 01667 464000

www.aberdeenairport.com, 03444 816666

www.scotrail.co.uk, 03448 110141

Local transport near the Moray Way is by bus. Stagecoach's route 10 connects Inverness, Elgin and Aberdeen on an hourly basis. Forres and Fochabers are the only places it serves on the Moray Way. Elgin, as the principal town in Moray, is the hub for Lossiemouth (20-minute service), also for hourly services to Burghead and Hopeman to the north, and for Rothes, Craigellachie, Dufftown and Aberlour to the south. There is also a less frequent service operated by Moray Council to Garmouth and Kingston. From Forres an hourly service operates to Findhorn, and an infrequent service runs from Elgin to Kinloss via Alves. In term-time a school bus run by Kineil Coaches serves Dunphail and Edinkillie.

In addition Moray Council operates a Dial-a-bus service within rural areas (phone 03001 234565) for which journeys must be booked on the previous day. Standard busfare rates apply.

There are no bus services between Grantown and Dava or between Grantown and Aberlour, although there are numerous taxi firms to be found in all the towns. The following provide guides to timetables:

www.stagecoachbus.co.uk, 01343 544222

Kineil Coaches, Elgin, 01343 552777

Deveron Coaches, Buckie, 01542 836363

Moray Council Dial-a-Bus, 0300 1234565

Traveline Scotland, 0871 2002233

A recently introduced tourist option is that of hiring electric bikes, a move in tune with a Low Carbon Transport initiative for travel between Carron and Craigellachie. Thanks to the Moray Car Share Club these can be rented at Forres, Findhorn, Aberlour and Lossiemouth. Contact *manager@moraycarshare.com* or telephone 01309 720120.

General travel information for the UK is available at *www.traveline.co.uk*.

Approximate Population Statistics for Towns and Villages on the Moray Way

If the circuit described in Sections 1–3 is followed, the following is the order of the towns and villages encountered, with their approximate populations:

Forres, 10,000
Kinloss, 1,000
Findhorn, 900
Burghead, 1,600
Hopeman, 1,600
Lossiemouth, 7,000
Kingston, 200
Garmouth, 400
Fochabers, 1,500
Craigellachie, 500
Aberlour, 1,000
Grantown, 2,400

THE MORAY WAY: key to the maps

Map and route category key

▬▬▬▬	Minor public roads
▬▪▬ ▬▪▬	Smoothly surfaced non motorised paths
▬ ▬ ▬ ▬ ▬	Broad track / forestry road
◉ ◉ ◉ ◉ ◉	Natural path
○ ○ ○ ○ ○ ○	Beach or dunes
▬▬ ▬▬	Primary road / 'A' road
══ ══	'B' road / minor road
◻◻◻◻◻◻◻▷	Track
─ ─ ─ ─ ─	Associated path
▬█1▬1█▬	National Cycle Route 1 - on road / off road
▬▬●──	Railway / main line station
	Woodland
	Greenspace
⌒	Beach
	Built up area
	River / loch
▨	Restricted area
🚌 1 per hour	Bus route / approximate frequency
▪▬▪▬▪▬	Cairngorms National Park boundary
Meikle Conval 569	Hill names - heights in metres

Map symbols key

P	Parking - free
P£	Parking - with charge
Ⓟ	Parking - possibly limited
👫	Public toilet
i	Visitor information centre
V	Visitor centre
🏛	Museum
♠	Distillery
✙	Church / abbey
🏰	Castle
18 9	Golf course (18/9 hole)
★	Other place of interest
◣	Local paths network
🚵	Mountain bike trail
⊟	Picnic site
☀	Lighthouse
✼	Viewpoint
⅄	Wind farm

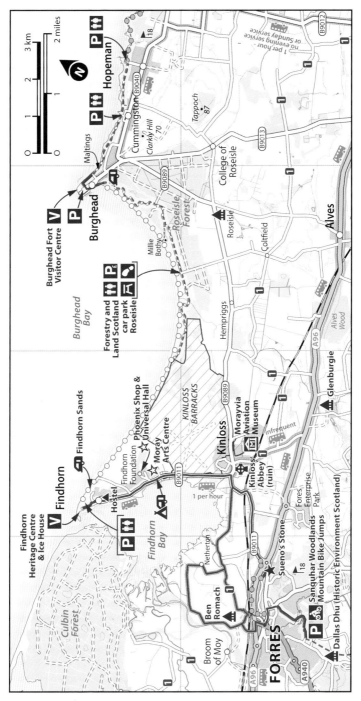

Moray Coast Trail: Forres to Hopeman.

1
THE MORAY COAST TRAIL

In Sections 1 to 3 route directions are highlighted in green type to separate these from information about features en route.

Forres

Forres is the largest town on the Moray Way and there is a good deal to see there for those prepared to pause awhile. Forres has been a Royal Burgh since David I signed a charter at some time around 1140. This is no longer extant but a subsequent charter signed by James IV in 1496 still exists, as is acknowledged in the name of a High Street café. The medieval street layout of a single thoroughfare with long narrow plots running at right angles to it is shown in the nineteenth-century map on p. 18, separated by closes or vennels, whose courses can still be traced in the lanes leading off the High Street.

Houses were gable-ended to the High Street, with each frontage precisely measured in Norman times as 1 rod (= 24 feet 9 inches/7.5 metres). The intention of its founders was that merchants should be brought to the town to occupy feus, build houses and promote commerce. The houses of that period were built of timber, mud and rubble, with doors and windows facing east and a windowless west wall where there was an access passage to divide each property from that of its neighbour. This style can still be observed in the property opposite St Leonard's church, even although it was rebuilt in the 1770s. No doubt each property had its dung heap at the far end from the house.

While Forres has always been a prosperous small town, there were periods within which the population increased greatly, the first between 1750 and 1790 when it went

Opposite: Hopeman Lodge on the Moray Coast Trail.

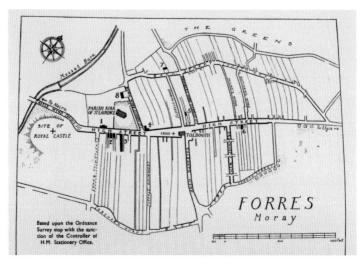

Nineteenth-century street plan of Forres.

up from around 2,000 to around 3,000, and the second between the 1950s and the present, when it has doubled to around 10,000. In the first of these periods exports and imports through Findhorn as its port (see p. 35) helped to ensure prosperity, while within the town itself its minister reported in the *Statistical Account* of 1793 that 'the inhabitants in general are disposed to industry'. Spinning linen yarn had for the previous twenty years or so brought in considerable amounts of money. The merchants sent the finished yarn to Glasgow where there was generally a ready sale, although a period of decline began in the mid-1840s due to the increased use of machinery in the south.

It is doubtful to what extent the common folk shared in this prosperity, although in financial terms they were better off by contrast with life in the hinterland. The *Statistical Account* goes on:

> Happy for our country did we keep pace in virtuous improvement, with the extravagant refinement in dress and manners. 30 years ago 30 shillings would have purchased a complete holiday suit of clothing for a labouring servant; according to the present mode of dress, it will require at least £5 to equip

him. In 1750 a servant engaged for harvest had 4 pence a day with his victuals, in 1790 10d. a day with two meals, that is 25 shillings for the whole time of harvest. A labouring man servant in 1790 had about £7 per year, a woman servant from £1 16s. to £2 2s.

The town's tradefolk at the time included 52 shoemakers, 25 weavers and 23 tailors, which makes a statement about the durability of eighteenth-century clothing and footwear!

By the 1800s most of the traditional buildings in the High Street had been replaced with permanent structures, and the first High Street fronts were created. Until 1975 Forres had its own centuries-old Town Council with a Provost

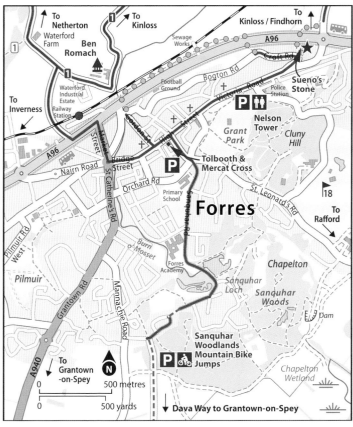

Forres today.

and bailies. This was dissolved by the Local Government Act of that year in favour of a single Council for the entire county of Moray. As in many similar towns, businesses have come and gone, some replaced by charity shops which use up to some extent the number of vacant properties of which there are almost invariably a few. Sadly the Falconer Museum, a nineteenth-century endowment to the town by Forres-born Hugh Falconer, was closed indefinitely in 2020 due to Council cutbacks, and its collections remain hidden from view. Hugh Falconer was a geologist, botanist, palaeontologist, evolutionist and friend of Charles Darwin. He became curator of the Botanic Gardens in Calcutta and agricultural adviser to the Indian Government, and was appointed a Fellow of the Royal Society.

The Council closures also included the Tourist Information Centre, although this sort of information is still available at the Town Hall which is under community ownership following a Community Asset Transfer from the Moray Council.

More details about Forres past and present are available in *A Forres Companion* by Norman Thomson (2015), costing £5 and available from the Washington bookshop in Forres, from Forres Town Hall or from Logie Steading (see p. 140). A very detailed account of Forres history is given in *The Annals of Forres* by Dr Robert Douglas (1936). If you locate a copy it is likely to be expensive.

A clockwise circuit of the Moray Way starting from Forres begins at the Tolbooth where you can either follow the official Moray Way route heading east out of the town, or head west, then north, on an alternative route. In either case you will come across two striking features in the centre of the High Street, which was voted in 2017 by the Scottish Towns Partnership to be the prettiest High Street in Scotland. These are:

Forres Tolbooth

The present Tolbooth complex was opened in 1849 to replace an earlier three-storey tower and courtroom. By

Forres Tolbooth and Mercat Cross.

this phase of building the present aspect of Forres town centre was largely established. Tolbooths were common throughout Scottish towns as places where councillors and magistrates met to formulate local policy and administer justice. A tolbooth included a jail, and in Forres the original cells still exist and can be visited between May and October – consult *www.forresheritage.co.uk* for details. The showpiece on such occasions is the lovingly restored courtroom, which functioned as such until as recently as 1975, when the Town Council was dissolved. The Tolbooth also has a railway room with a model of the demolished station (see p. 194) and photographs of early days on the Dava and Aberdeen lines.

Forres Mercat Cross

This miniature version of the Scott Monument in Edinburgh was erected in 1844, on the site of the previous Mercat Cross, which itself had replaced an earlier megalithic stone pillar reported to have been 20 feet (6 metres) high. Like similar Mercat Crosses throughout Scotland

Carving on the Mercat Cross.

it would have been used for royal and civic proclamations, as well as having manacles ('jougs') attached to it in which prisoners were chained for crimes which fell short of meriting execution or burning at the stake. The ornamental corner pillars have fallen off from time to time, but a project in 2021 replaced some of them and restored the cross to its original glory. Some of the small carvings are worth a glance, such as the one illustrated here – a story in stone long forgotten! A time capsule from 1844 is buried in the base.

From the Tolbooth and Mercat Cross open area the official route heads east along Victoria Road. The most notable features here are:

Forres in Bloom Displays in the Grant Park

From June to October it is impossible not to stop and admire the flower beds, planted and maintained by enthusiastic volunteers, which have established a national reputation for the town. A board at the entrance to the park details years of prize-winning, culminating in two Entente Florale Europe gold awards, together with a Beautiful Scotland medium-sized town Gold Award in 2021. The park itself was gifted to the town in 1924 by Sir Alexander Grant, a native of Forres who rose from being a baker's boy to the chairmanship of the biscuit company McVitie and Price. A sunken garden is close to the entrance board, and is a striking feature created on the site of what used to be Sir Alexander's mansion house in the park, but which burnt down in 1940. Forres in Bloom, a long-established and well-supported volunteer organisation, also maintains the flowerbeds, barrels and baskets throughout the High Street and elsewhere in the town.

St John's Episcopal Church

This church, with its unmistakable campanile-like tower and wheel window, was designed in 1841 by Patrick Wilson and Thomas Mackenzie, who also designed the Mercat Cross. It is the oldest extant church building in Forres and is normally open during the day. It contains three fine wall-sized murals dated 1906, 1912 and 1936.

Nelson Tower

Peeping above the trees on the summit of Cluny Hill, this octagonal tower was built by the Trafalgar Club, an organisation consisting largely of Forres businessmen and gentry, to commemorate Nelson's victory in 1805. It was was completed in 1812 but was handed over to the Town

The Nelson Tower.

Council in 1843 when the club ran out of money and support. Trafalgar is popularly but mistakenly thought of as
an English triumph – this monument is a reminder of the
part Scotland played by providing timber for the ships,
as well as five ships' captains and almost a third of the
sailors, who were recruited from Scottish fishing towns
and villages. The tower is reached by going up the hill
in the Grant Park and can be climbed inside to get good
views of Findhorn and the Moray Firth. It is manned by
volunteers from Forres Heritage Trust, and is normally
open seven days a week between 2 and 4 pm from April
to September. Admission is by donation to the Trust.

The Witches Stone

A boulder with a plaque on the south side of Victoria Road
immediately opposite the Ramnee Hotel marks the spot
where, in the seventeenth century, spiked barrels containing women condemned as witches came to rest after being
rolled down the hill as a preliminary to burning. Or so it
is said! What is certainly true is that in the second half of
the century, no organisation was more zealous than the
Church of Scotland in hunting out ugly old women who
were believed to have sold their souls to Satan, thereby
deserving death. The then Bishop of Moray, Reverend
Murdo Mackenzie, was particularly notable for his zeal
in detecting witches, who were then handed over to the
civil authorities for execution. The penalty was carried out
either by hanging on the town gibbet on what is now the
Elgin road, or by burning – the latter being the preference
of the Town Council because it was cheaper!

Turn left down a side road (Findhorn Road) leading to
the pedestrian/cycle bridge over the A96 Forres bypass.
Just before you reach the bridge pause to wonder at . . .

Sueno's Stone

Sueno's Stone is a remarkable 23-foot (7 metre) high
carved monument, unique in Scotland for the extraordinary detail of the carving by the unknown craftsmen who

Sueno's Stone, detail of third panel.

created elaborate battle scenes on one side and a cross, together with other Celtic ornamentation, in relief on the other, as well as Celtic knotwork on the edges. Originally discovered lying flat, then partially lifted, it was fully raised and set into its stepped plinth in the late eighteenth century by Lady Anne Campbell, Countess of Moray. Nobody knows how much of it lies unseen below the ground. There is general agreement that both the sandstone and its base came from some distance away, probably the Clashach quarry area of Hopeman (see p. 51). The stone may have been conveyed by sea, the level of which was higher than it is today. Was it carved horizontally and then raised? An open question. Centuries of burial before its discovery in the eighteenth century have, fortunately for us, preserved its carvings. In the early 1990s, Historic Environment Scotland enclosed it in a glass case for protection, much needed as the weathering of the carvings in the last two decades or so has been dramatic.

What was its purpose? It must surely commemorate some significant event, and yet it is remarkable that there is no documentary evidence about its origins. There can be little doubt that it describes a battle scene, as around twenty soldiers are depicted, as well as seven decapitated victims whose severed heads may well be the objects illustrated under the bridge (or is it a bell? or even a broch?) in the third panel down. Several plausible alternative theories have been put forward concerning its origins, of which the following is a summary (see 'Sueno's Stone and its interpreters' in *Moray: Province and People* by David Sellar, Scottish Society for Northern Studies, 1998).

Sueno was a Danish (at that time a generic term for all Scandinavians) war leader whose army defeated the Scots under King Malcolm II (reigned 1005-1034) at the Battle of Forres (1008). Malcolm achieved his revenge at the Battle of Mortlach (1010) where the Danes were decisively defeated. Sweyn the Forkbeard, father of Canute, was King of Denmark at this time and it is possible that he was this Sueno.

Another theory suggests that it may commemorate a victory by Kenneth McAlpin, the first king of Alba, that is of Scotland (reigned 842-858 AD) over the Picts, or perhaps a later battle in 880 when Sigurd the Powerful, Earl of Orkney, defeated the Scots led by Malbride the Bucktooth. Yet another battle that it might commemorate is documented in ancient chronicles. In it King Dubh or Duff (reigned 962-966 AD) was killed by the Men of Moray at Forres. Possibly it is his body which reportedly lay under the bridge at Kinloss and which is depicted as lying under a bridge in the third panel down. There are several corpses lying under this bridge (if indeed that is what it is) together with decapitated corpses to left and right.

From Sueno's Stone proceed over the foot/cycle bridge and carry on along the pavement alongside the B9011 until you reach the traffic lights at Kinloss.

Alternative Routes from Forres

These routes start along the High Street, heading towards the handsome and much photographed St Laurence Church built in 1906 to replace a decaying 1775 church on a site which has been a place of Christian worship continuously since Alexander III built a chapel by Forres Castle in 1175 as a memorial to his wife Margaret.

Interior of St Laurence Church.

The church is spacious and light, and boasts an outstanding collection of fourteen Douglas Strachan stained glass windows. It is frequently open to visitors during the months May to October.

Almost opposite St Laurence Church lies the façade of the former Castlehill Church which united with St Leonard's in 1972. This is currently being restored as a private residence. A short distance beyond that and just past the Post Office, metal gates lead to a 'Cleopatra's needle' (the Thomson Monument) on the Forres Ridge, the site of Forres Castle in medieval times. The monument is a tribute to a philanthropic surgeon in the Crimean War who died young abroad, having treated friends and foes alike. He hailed from Cromarty and had no direct connection with Forres. His family were in dispute with the Cromarty laird at the time, but thanks to the esteem in which he was held by the army's medical director, this alternative site was chosen to commemorate him.

For those on foot, do not proceed further down the High Street, but retreat to the junction with Gordon Street, and continue along Gordon Street until it ceases to be a motor road, at which point continue straight ahead down a path which leads to a crossing of the Forres bypass and a signpost indicating the Moray Coast Trail. Be prepared to encounter some recent chainsaw artistry as you go. The path runs alongside the railway, passes the sewage works, then on the left the nurseries of Christies-Elite, the wholesale arm of a business founded in 1920 whose fame and reputation has spread far beyond Forres. It supplies around 1.5 million seedlings, both conifers and broad-leaf, which are sold annually to estates and forestry enterprises all over the UK. At this point the path takes a turn and you have to cross the Forres bypass (A96). The path continues for a short distance until you come to a metalled road. Turn left and follow the tarmac into Croft Road, which leads you to Sueno's Stone.

For those cycling, continue down the High Street. The road goes downhill, crossing the Mosset Burn by a bridge of 1908. At the Victoria Hotel proceed down Tytler Street, named after a former Forres property owner, on which you pass a ruin which is all that remains of the former Corn Exchange. Built in 1867, it later became a theatre and dance hall, then a cattle mart, and finally Hamilton's auction house whose regular sales were a well-known Forres institution. On the right is the former Royal Hotel, once the grandest hotel in the town after the Forres Hydro. It closed in the 1990s and then became a hostel for the homeless. The Forres Hydro, which lies on the south side of Cluny Hill, was built as a huge railway hotel, and became famed internationally for the curative power of Forres's woods and climate. It is now provides residential accommodation for participants in the programmes of the Findhorn Foundation (see p. 32).

At the end of Tytler Street dismount and follow a short path which takes you to where you cross the A96 (Forres bypass) and head along the branch road towards Waterford. Cross over the bridge, which was constructed when the railway was realigned in 2017 with the present Forres station lying to your right. The site of the previous station is on the left, but all trace of it has been absorbed into an industrial estate. At the next road junction turn right to join NCN1 (National Cycling Network 1). After a quarter of a mile you pass Benromach distillery (see p. 182). NCN1 continues along the road leading to Kinloss. If you turn left rather than right an alternative minor public road via Netherton Farm takes you to a good spot for watching birds on the edge of the bay. Findhorn Bay is nationally important for migrating birds and waders, and has the status of a Local Nature Reserve. It is also an area favoured by wildfowlers, and there has been much controversy over the exercise of their sport clashing with the rights of residents along the bay, and lovers of the Nature Reserve. In the last century, local wildfowlers and nature lovers managed to coexist in more or less mutual tolerance. However in recent years wildfowlers from as far afield as the north of England started to arrive in considerable numbers, leaving litter and wounded birds behind, and in extreme cases threatening local ramblers and dog walkers.

In 2016 a series of interpretation boards were put in place both around the bay and within Findhorn and the dunes. These are an excellent help in identifying the great variety of birds which can be observed by those with patience (and binoculars!) to do so. Every board has an overview map giving the locations of all the others.

All of the above routes out of Forres converge at Kinloss, home to one of Moray's most notable ecclesiastical ruins, namely:

Kinloss Abbey

The name Kinloss is said to be derived (just about plausibly!) from 'king lost', the lost king in question being King David I on a hunting expedition in 1150 or so. This misadventure inspired him to found the Abbey there. Be that as it may, the Abbey itself is real and its historical importance has in recent times been greatly underestimated, not least for its royal associations. Edward I, Edward III and Mary Queen of Scots were all accommodated here for seven, fourteen and three nights respectively. But for the combination of internal corruption and the Protestant reforming

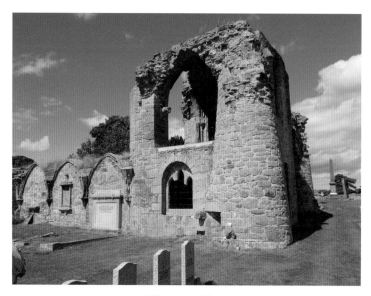

Kinloss Abbey.

zeal of the mid-sixteenth century, this might well have been one of the most magnificent religious buildings in the United Kingdom, both in architecture and scale. A major phase in the development of the buildings and creation of the library and fruit orchard is attributable to Robert Reid, its most notable abbot who was in charge from 1528 to 1553. He later became Bishop of Orkney, ambassador of King James V to the courts of England and France and President of the Court of Session, and left a bequest in his will to found a college in Edinburgh which later became Edinburgh University.

Following the Reformation much of the Abbey's land was sold off to the more financially astute Brodies of Lethen. The Laird Alexander Brodie caused the magnificent church buildings to be demolished, and the stones sold to Oliver Cromwell's minions who used them to help construct the short-lived Citadel at Inverness.

The Kinloss Abbey Trust was formed in 2003 and its members have undertaken the considerable task of restoring the Abbot's House, in the course of which they have revealed a sixteenth-century Scottish tower house of some grandeur, reflecting the high status of the Abbot. Free guided tours take place at 2 pm on the last Sunday in each of the summer months. The care of the Abbey itself is in the hands of Historic Environment Scotland who have installed several informative interpretation boards.

At the cost of a deviation from the Way of a mile or so, those with an interest in aviation in World War II and after, or in astronomy, will not be disappointed by a visit to Morayvia.

Morayvia Aviation Museum and Planetarium

In 2011 a group of aviation enthusiasts who had at one time or another been based at RAF Kinloss formed the Nimrod Heritage Group to ensure that what had gone on there should not be forgotten. They started a campaign to establish a museum which opened in 2014 and recorded the history of the airbase and the aeroplanes which had operated there during World War II and afterwards (see p. 39 for more detail). This is now one of the premier military museums in Scotland. Features

Part of the Morayvia collection (photo by Bob Pultney).

include a fully equipped Nimrod fuselage and cockpit, three complete helicopters, plus cockpits of numerous other aircraft, along with many other exhibits relating to World War II in the air. A cinema and a planetarium have regular showings during opening hours. The site of the museum was formerly a primary school and is in the midst of the urban village estate which formerly provided married quarters for the air base. For opening times and directions see *www.morayvia.org.uk* or Facebook, or tel: 01309 691916.

Proceed from Kinloss to Findhorn by turning onto the B9011 and after a short distance you will see Kinloss parish church on your right.

Kinloss Church

This building, which now fulfils the dual role of church and village hall, was originally built in 1765 with the tower being added in 1830. It is reputed to have been the first church in the north of Scotland to install an organ, in 1879. Currently it is in a four-way linkage with other churches in Burghead, Alves and Findhorn.

As you continue to Findhorn, you pass the runways of the Kinloss airbase on your right (see p. 39), and shortly after that come to the bird hide adjoining the B9011 which gives good views over Findhorn Bay and has a good interpretation board. Because of repeated vandalism, access to the hide is restricted. Almost directly opposite the hide lies the entrance to the Park, home to the world-famous Findhorn Foundation.

The Findhorn Foundation

It is worth turning right into the Park, where the first building you encounter is the Phoenix shop, notable for its interesting and carefully selected food specialities, as well as a range of high-quality art items, and books about the 'one-world eco-village' philosophy which inspired Peter and Eileen Caddy and Dorothy MacLean to set up the Foundation in 1962. At the time it was perceived in the neighbourhood, depending on one's point of view, as either a profoundly spiritual community or a hippy commune. At the roundabout just beyond the shop, turn right into the Field of Dreams, the site of around forty houses, most with unique and intriguing design features and with different variants of brightly painted wood cladding, As you return to the main road through the Park, the largest building you see is the hexagon shaped Universal Hall, which serves the entire local area as a concert hall, open-plan theatre and cinema. Further on there is an estate of more recently built houses of a conventional pattern, but still embodying the notion of sustainability and environmental harmony which inspired the original settlement. A path leads off to Cullerne Gardens, part of the Foundation where the legendary giant vegetables grew which, according to local folklore, caused Californians to flood here in awe and wonderment in the 1960s.

Having visited or passed by the Foundation, it is not long before you reach the first houses of . . .

Findhorn Village

As with other towns on the Moray Way, there is no single definitive route through Findhorn. To see something of how Findhorn came to be what it is now, a walk round the streets and lanes which connect the former fishermen's cottages at the village's heart can prove rewarding.

The present Findhorn village can be dated very exactly. By 1702 its inhabitants completed what had been a gradual withdrawal from its predecessor village, as winds, tides and shifting sands threatened their homes. The earlier village was built at the furthest north point on the east side of the bay called the E'e.

Some sources claim Findhorn is the third village to bear the name, perhaps erroneously assuming that the seventeenth-century destruction of the nearby Barony of Culbin by shifting sands in 1694 resulted in an even earlier relocation.

Findhorn village and bay.

Until the twentieth century, fishing was the dominant way of life for Findhorn's inhabitants. The *Statistical Account of Scotland* in the 1790s recounts that the river abounded with salmon, which in the spring and beginning of summer were boiled, packed in 'kits', that is cylindrical wooden vessels with lids, and bound with staves. Around 300 such barrels were sent to the London market by ship annually, where they fetched four pence per pound compared with the one penny or one and a half pence a pound which the local diet of haddock, whiting, cod, eels, flounders and skate fetched at Forres. This source of prosperity was briefly halted when Findhorn Bay was flooded to a width of a mile in 1782, which was also a year of general famine and failed harvests. Later, in the course of the great Moray floods of 1829, waters again covered everywhere between Findhorn and Forres, and Findhorn fishing boats are reported to have helped rescue numerous grateful Forres residents.

As you enter the village itself, a low ridge on the bay side of the road clearly traces out the line of the nineteenth-century railway (see p. 197).

Findhorn itself is a magnet for yachting enthusiasts. The Royal Findhorn Yacht Club has its headquarters in the former Findhorn House built in 1775 which also houses the Piers Café. Findhorn's bars – the Kimberley, the Crown and Anchor (built in 1739 and the oldest extant house in the village) and the Captain's Table – are full of life throughout the summer season. A water-taxi service takes visitors across the mouth of the bay to land in Culbin Forest on its eastern side, a spot which is popular for picnics. There are two piers – on the south pier the Mercat Cross is said to date from 1703 and to have been built from stone carried from the old town. The Old Station House marks the former railway terminus, while on the south pier inch-proud studs of two parallel rail tracks can be traced leading to the docked ships.

Turn right at the Crown and Anchor, then left to follow signs to two neighbouring buildings on the route which are well worth visiting. In both cases entry is by donation.

The Findhorn Ice House

This is one of the oldest icehouses in the UK, where winter ice harvested from the river Findhorn was processed on a commercial scale to make possible the storing and despatch of bay-caught salmon to every part of the kingdom from the shore-based salmon fisheries which lasted until the 1980s.

The reconstruction of the Ice House and displays have made this a particularly fascinating mini-museum.

Findhorn Heritage Centre

This excellent little museum lies immediately opposite the Ice House, and packs into an amazingly compact space the history both of the regional geography and its social development.

In the seventeenth century Findhorn was the principal seaport of Moray and vessels regularly sailed across the North Sea as far afield as the Baltic, exporting timber, grain, hides, beef and salmon, and importing coal, brandy, fine wines, muslin and spices. The narrow and shallow entrance to the Bay and the constantly changing

Sunset on Findhorn Bay.

bar created obstacles to navigation, and as the size of trading vessels increased, so the volume of trade to the village declined. The last nail in the coffin was the coming of the railways in the nineteenth century.

In 1746 Findhorn Bay was the last training ground and centre of resistance for the Jacobites prior to the battle of Culloden. In March 1746 they commandeered all the available fishing boats along the Moray coast to launch an initially successful amphibious operation to land at Dornoch and scatter the government troops stationed in Sutherland and Caithness. Also in that month a French brigantine, *Le Bien Trouvé*, entered the tidal waters with dispatches for Bonnie Prince Charlie. Although her route of departure was blockaded by two British warships, she managed to slip away under cover of darkness. Even as late as April 1746 the remnants of the Jacobite army were drilling in Findhorn as the Duke of Cumberland swept all before him in his advance on Culloden.

The early twentieth century saw a decline in fishing as the traditional two-masted Zulus were replaced by larger vessels. Some Zulus were temporarily beached on the western shore of the Bay when their crews went to fight in the First World War. They were never used again, and their decaying skeletons are still visible at low tide on the west shore of the bay. The Zulu took its name from the Zulu war that was raging in South Africa in 1879. The Zulu boats were invented by William Campbell, a Lossiemouth fisherman who was the first to introduce this form of fishing boat. His own boat, the *Nonesuch*, had the characteristic vertical stem and steeply raked stern. They were popular in Lossiemouth and their fame spread along the whole Moray coast. They were big and fast, which helped reduce the time taken from the fishing grounds to market.

Before leaving Findhorn it is worth going as far out towards the Moray Firth as the very considerable tide range will allow. Grey seals can often be spotted on the sandbank and on the Culbin side in great numbers, and their 'singing' is a distinctive sound which can often be heard in the village. A group of identical beach huts were built by a private developer in 2017 not far from the entrance to the bay. The private ownership of this part of the beach created a great deal of division amongst permanent residents in the village.

From Findhorn shore proceed eastwards either on the shore or among the dunes, where you will be treading underfoot a three-quarters of a mile-long wall of thousands of tons of rocks from local quarries which were dumped as a foreshore barrier against future coastal erosion, following the hurricane which hit the area in February 1983. There are numerous groynes and stepped pathways leading from the dunes to the beach.

Burghead Bay

Looking eastward from Findhorn on a calm day, it is hard to believe that in the year or more following July 1940 this was an intensely militarised area, due to the perceived

Path to Burghead.

probability of a German invasion. Frantic activity by local contractors was undertaken, so that by October 1940 the seven-mile beach from Findhorn to Burghead had anti-aircraft stakes planted along its whole length just below the high water mark. The stubs of some of these are still visible at low tide. Concrete blocks (cubes) were placed just above the high water mark, together with pillboxes accommodating machine-guns and anti-tank guns, the majority of which were on Innes Links (see p. 65). The rings on the top surface of some of the cubes were there to secure rolls of barbed wire.

There are two main types of pillbox on the Moray coast: some, known as Type 24, are in the form of truncated hexagons with three gun embrasures facing the sea; others, known as Type 26, are square or rectangular. Kinloss was a major bomber aerodrome supported by a satellite aerodrome at Rosevalley which lay inland from the easternmost part of the bay, and of which no remains survive.

Interestingly, no coastal defences were constructed between Burghead and Lossiemouth, which must have left some possible tank landing sites exposed on either side of Hopeman.

Setting out eastwards from Findhorn on the seven-mile journey around Burghead Bay, pause and look at Burghead in the distance and consider how in aeons past this journey could have been made in a straight line. The relentless tides have carved out the bay and continue to do so. The dunes and shingle storm edge system from Nairn to Burghead is the largest such complex in Scotland. Every so often huge dust-storms blow in from the sea, skimming soil off the fields and reducing visibility to zero. In the 1730s a massive tree-planting scheme was started to stabilise these shifting dunes. As you leave Findhorn and before reaching the forest, you will see Kinloss airfield fenced off to your right.

Building on the RAF Kinloss site started in 1937, displacing seven farms, although the permanent runways were not completed until 1942. The RAF station opened on 1 April 1939 and served as 14 Flying Training School at the beginning of the Second World War, followed by 19 Operational Training Unit (OTU) which trained and operated bomber crews on Whitleys and Ansons. RAF Kinloss was used as a base for attacks in the Norwegian area, including those by Flying Fortresses and Lancaster bombers against the battleships *Admiral Scheer* and *Tirpitz* in 1941 and 1942 and again in 1944 when *Tirpitz* was finally sunk.

In July 1945 19 OTU was disbanded and RAF Kinloss was handed over to Coastal Command, thereby beginning RAF Kinloss's long association with maritime reconnaissance operations. The wartime Avro Lancaster bomber was adapted for anti-submarine and rescue duties and also watching for Russian ships and submarines in the seas around Norway. Neptune aircraft were based at Kinloss, and from 1959 Shackletons, which continued in service until they in turn were replaced by Nimrods in 1971. Nimrods served in the Falklands conflict in 1982 and in the Gulf wars in 1991 and 2003. Until 2010 RAF Kinloss was the main base for the RAF's fleet of Nimrod MR2 maritime patrol aircraft; however after the Ministry of Defence's cancellation of its MRA4 replacement, Kinloss was no longer required by the RAF and regular flying operations ceased on 31 July 2011, involving the redeployment of 2,500 RAF personnel and their families. On 26 July 2012 the RAF ensign was lowered for the last time, and replaced by the flag of 39 Engineer Regiment (Air Support). The runways are currently maintained as a relief landing site for RAF Lossiemouth.

After it starts about a mile east of the easternmost part of Findhorn dunes, Roseisle Forest presents itself as a combination of forest park and superb beach. From its centre the walker has options for reaching Burghead, either by a beach walk (possibly on shingle at high tide), a forestry walk, or a combination of the two.

Roseisle

Roseisle is a recreational park managed by Forestry and Land Scotland (formerly the Forestry Commission) and is well waymarked. There is an interpretation centre with toilets at the midpoint of the bay and refreshments can be obtained at high season. This can also be a convenient intermediate access point to the Moray Way for walkers or cyclists who can reach it from the B9089. There is an extensive car park for which a small charge is made.

Approaching Burghead along the beach there is another huge line of concrete blocks with pillboxes at crazy angles roughly 600 yards apart. At low tide you can also see the remains of the anti-aircraft posts mentioned earlier, which were concreted in on the seaward side of the tank blocks. The forest route eastwards from the Forestry and Land Scotland car park is well defined. It became known as the Burma Road by the Second World War troops who trained there for the D-Day landings, and still retains that name. Between the car park and Burghead is a clearing, offering something of a mini-landscape between sea and forest. This can be approached either from the beach where the Millie Burn is crossed, or from a side path on the Burma Road, reached 200 yards or so after crossing the burn on a culvert. In the clearing lies the ruined Millie Bothy, once a two-storeyed salmon fishermen's station.

D-Day Practice Sites at Roseisle

1944 saw a second period of intense activity in which Burghead Bay became a practice area for the D-Day landings. It was chosen for testing tanks and amphibious vehicles, because of its similarity to the terrain in Normandy. Farmers around the area were given just three weeks to evacuate their farms, and this posed considerable logistic problems, particularly as all activity had to be kept secret. Few people in Forres knew what was going on. Corners on the then narrow roads had to be widened to allow tanks to manoeuvre. Army units set out from the Black Isle and came across the Firth to 'invade' the evacuated area. Landing craft rolled over farmland, through fences and dykes, creating havoc and damaging drains and buildings. Looking at the closely packed trees, a mixture of russet-barked Scots and grey-barked Corsican pine, it is easy to see how this massive area of forests and dunes was nicknamed 'the Burma Road'.

A semi-hexagonal pillbox near Burghead.

41

Beneath the surface of the bay lie the remains of eight Vanguard tanks, a model which proved unsuccessful and superseded by the Sherman tank, the type used in the D-Day invasion. The driver of one of the Vanguards was buried in his vehicle off Culbin, which means that this area of the Moray Firth is technically a war grave.

From Roseisle the signposted Moray Way follows a clear main track. As Burghead is reached it proceeds through the caravan park and reaches the main entrance. From here, turning right, it leads eventually to Park Street, which crosses the neck of the Burghead peninsula alongside the huge Maltings. However a diversion to the village is well rewarded. A principal attraction is the:

Burghead Pictish Fort and Visitor Centre

The Heritage Centre overlooking the Moray Firth at the apex of the Pictish site is run by the Burghead Headland Trust and is notable both for its displays and its views, and, especially in winter and spring, as an observation point for seabirds.

The extent of the fort is extraordinary and the visitor centre in its Martello-like tower spells out in detail the amazing archaeological items which have been discovered as illustrated in its model reconstructing what the fort must have looked like, with ramparts eight metres thick

Reconstruction of Burghead Pictish fort
(photo by Gordon Noble).

and six metres high. These also include an ancient well in the village discovered in 1809 and named after St Aethan, a follower of St Columba. A key can be obtained from a nearby house and you climb down 22 steps to view it.

The site of the Pictish Fort was always a prominent feature of the headland, debate having taken place in the past about whether it was the the place called *Pronoton* on Ptolemy's Roman map or what the Vikings called *Torfness*. There is little doubt the Picts were responsible for the vast scale of the fort and buildings, protected by high walls and ramparts, the outlines of which remain clearly visible today (see the artist's impression of what it would have looked like, opposite). The round structure which most visitors think of as the 'fort' today was, in fact, a signal station dating back to c. 500 AD, and later a coastguard lookout. The area landward from this covering about four acres was divided into two unequal terraces. The smaller upper one was the preserve of royalty and religious leaders; the larger one below housed the lower ranks who served their superiors above.

The Visitor Centre opened in 2003 in the old signal station and entailed a huge amount of sensitive building work undertaken to the high standards of Historic Environment Scotland. In 2013 a viewing room on a lower level allowing panoramic views out to sea was carved out of the high cliff on which the Visitor Centre stands. This is open from April to September, manned by volunteers. There is no charge but donations are requested. On 11 January each year the Clavie, a flaming tar bucket whose burning embers were the Pictish answer to antibiotics, is paraded around the village in a big public ceremony.

The most distinctive birds which can be seen at close quarters in the winter months at Burghead are the long-tailed ducks which regularly swim in the harbour. Elsewhere in the Firth they are usually only to be seen flying at speed over the sea. Red-throated divers are regularly sighted in winter (with binoculars!) anywhere from Burghead eastwards, and red-breasted mergansers are also reasonably common. Purple-headed sandpipers sometimes scurry about in the rocks. Huge rafts of both eiders and scoters can sometimes be seen offshore. By contrast, sightings of dolphins, although much discussed in the tourist literature, require a combination of luck, persistence and keen eyesight which is not often the case for folk whose primary objective is walking.

Burghead Harbour

Burghead Harbour was designed by Thomas Telford as part of his Scottish harbours project. It was opened in 1809, with William Young who had earlier founded Hopeman (see p. 46) as sole shareholder. In the harbour basin, look for the bedding planes where rock was hewn out to create the harbour.

After the building of the harbour, vigorous trade similar to that of Findhorn in both cargoes and destinations was very successful in reviving local businesses. Also, by the 1840s, passenger boats called regularly *en route* to and from Inverness, Leith, Aberdeen, and even every second Monday, to London. Initially travellers were transported ashore from big ships to smaller ones, however the break-water extension in 1858 allowed the larger vessels to call at the outer quay. A ferry service ran across the Moray Firth until the 1870s when rail traffic began to supersede travel by sea. The harbour is still commercially active with fishing vessels. The surrounding granaries used by

A long-tailed duck.

Aerial view of Burghead (photo by Gordon Noble).

nineteenth-century traders have now been largely now converted into flats, but their distinctive contribution to the harbour landscape has preserved much of the nineteenth-century ambience.

A recently revealed secret of the Second World War is that the Old Salmon Bothy at the harbour was the mainland headquarters of the Shetland Bus project. A memorial on the harbourside commemorates the gallant Norwegian fishermen who lost their lives in this operation, ferrying men, supplies and weapons from Shetland across to resistance fighters in Norway. For a full account of this, see *The Shetland Bus* by David Howarth (1951).

Superstitions

The fishing folk in Burghead had many superstitions — seeing a nun or a crow or a black cat on the way to the boats meant turning back, as did the sight of a rat on the shore, or the women giving their menfolk a wave, which meant that a sea wave would envelop the boats. Anybody whistling had an equally disastrous potential. One wonders how they ever got off to work at all! Once the fishermen were under way, the teapot must not be emptied on board for fear of capsizing the boat, eggshells must be crushed to prevent witches using them as boats, plus many more superstitious precautions.

On a more practical level, illustrated by surviving photographs, was the custom of the womenfolk piggy-backing the menfolk and wading with them from the shore to the boats to prevent the men's clothes being soaked prematurely. A strong breed of women indeed – perhaps their Pictish blood was responsible!

As with Hopeman, the Free Church of Scotland was the dominant religious denomination in the area following the disruption of 1843.

The Maltings which you come to next is by far the most prominent building in Burghead. Built in 1967 on the site of an old ropeworks and owned by Diageo, the Maltings takes in over 100 million kilograms of barley per year and produces in return over 85 million kilograms of malted, that is germinated, barley. (It takes one kilogram of malted barley to make a bottle of Scottish whisky.) In the past most distilleries had their own malting floors but this is no longer the case.

The route from Burghead to Hopeman is an obvious former railway track. Halfway between Burghead and Hopeman the village of Cummingston looks down on the Trail, where there is also a car park, play area and bicycle maintenance post. There are some cliffs here which are favoured by rock climbers, and there is also a cave worth peeping into. Hopeman Station is now the base for the extensive caravan and mobile home park, called appropriately West Sands, which is the first group of dwellings encountered on entering the village. The caravan park features the somewhat incongruous sight of a double-decker bus, which in the holiday season serves as a popular takeaway café for residents of and visitors to the site.

Hopeman Village

The first houses of the village were built in 1806 on land bought by William Young of Inverugie as a commercial venture. In 1818 it became established as a fishing port, and between 1836 and 1838 the harbour was created to

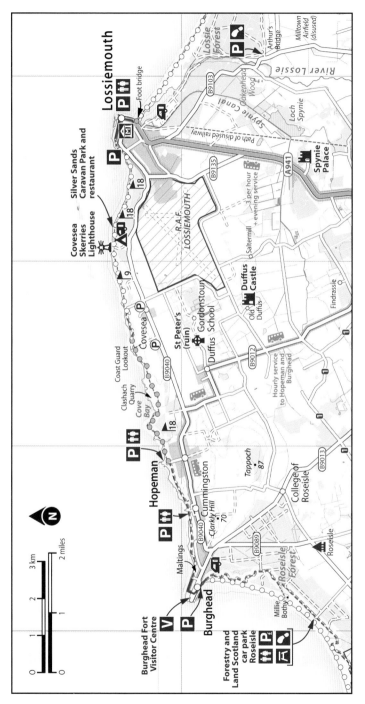

Moray Coast Trail central, Burghead to Lossiemouth.

Aerial view of Hopeman village.

export stone from local quarries. It was not until 1854 that a church was built in Hopeman to serve a congregation of the Free Church of Scotland, whose support from the largely fishing community of the village was strong. In 1911 the interior was completely remodelled, and its prominent church tower was added in 1923 thanks to a generous gift by Innes Cameron, an Elgin distiller. In 1929 the church, along with the majority of Free Churches joined the Church of Scotland. The church is now linked with those of Duffus and Spynie.

Across the road from the West Sands caravan park there is an armillary (large sundial) sitting atop an 1860s ice house, opposite which is the former railway station (see p. 193) recently restored to its near original condition as the reception block for the caravan park.

When it was first founded, Gaelic-speaking families from as far afield as Campbeltown came to settle in Hopeman which had a large fleet of fishing boats – forty drifters and thirty-six sail boats – superseded later by line and seine boats. For several years Hopeman had the largest average catch of all the Moray fishing stations.

Until the 1970s Hopeman remained a fishing town, and freshly landed fish could be purchased at the harbour. Most of the boat crews at that time fished what were then the more lucrative waters off the west coast, and cars with crews departing on Sunday evenings and returning on Thursdays were a familiar sight. Nowadays North Sea fishing is the preferred option. The more highly equipped boats that fish there are based at Peterhead to which crews travel by minibus, staying at sea for five to ten days at a time.

The six miles from Hopeman to Lossiemouth are full of features. Start from the harbour which is now dominated by pleasure craft and by a restored crane, brought from Wick and in use until the 1970s. As you proceed eastwards, Hopeman School stands high above the recreation ground, and a small monument at the end of the ridge houses a millenium time capsule. A colourful line of beach huts testifies to the popularity and attractiveness of Sheepey's Bay, where those who don't totally dismiss the possibility of sea-witches should warn over-adventurous children about the dangers of falling into the clutches of of the Grin Iron Wife!

Normally there is a week in July in which a large marquee on the recreation ground becomes the focus of Hopeman Gala week. To the east the large building standing high called Hopeman Lodge (see p. 16) is now privately owned. It was originally a summer home for Admiral Duff, then later a boarding house for Gordonstoun School, and still later self-catering flats. Daisy Rock beckons invitingly to the north of the path for a quick scramble. If you look directly north to the rock, the cleft indicates more or less accurately the point at which the midsummer sun sets. A little further along to the south the 15th green of Hopeman golf course comes almost down to path level. A short distance round the point the 12th green does come down to path level – a hole that the former Open Champion Paul Lawrie described as the best short hole in Scotland.

Gorse taking over between the sea and the golf course has increased, and magnificent though the display is at its peak in May, characteristic spring plants such as spring beauty (*Claytonia perforiata*) and scurvy grass (*Cochlearia*), although still present, are being overwhelmed. Stonechats are common as they flit from branch to branch. Unwelcome visitors in the form of mink can be seen in the water anywhere between Burghead and Lossiemouth. Having been brought to the UK from America for their fur, some escaped in the 1930s and started to breed here in the wild, where they attack salmon, frogs, ground-nesting seabirds and water voles, into whose tunnels mink can squeeze themselves. Another unwelcome source of trouble is the periodic gorse fires, which in a short period of time can transform a floral yellow spectacle into a blackened hillside.

After climbing a few steps and with Hopeman Golf Course on the left, look down into Cove Bay, a favourite spot for picnics and wild camping. Most notable however is a very clear example of a geological fault. After a short distance the path meets the Clashach Quarry road. At this point there is a possible diversion inland which those with a penchant for historic ruins might like to consider. If you choose to do so the cliff top path can be resumed by going through the locked and gated Quarry road from where it leaves the junction of the B9040 and the B9012 and continuing until it meets the coastal trail.

Diversion

Nearby are two significant monuments in the care of Historic Environment Scotland. The ruined Duffus Castle is one of the finest examples in Scotland of a motte and bailey castle, built by a nobleman called Freskin of whom little is known other than that one of his forebears fought with David I on his Scottish incursions. This dates the first building of the castle to the twelfth century and this was followed shortly afterwards by the founding of St Peter's

Kirk, whose eighteenth-century rebuilding was on a vast scale for what was a small parish. It has numerous carved gentry stones in the graveyard.

Assuming you have not chosen this diversion, turn left at the path/quarry road junction, and after a short distance you come to . . .

Clashach Quarry

This quarry has had a colourful life in more senses than one. Its sandstone boulders, laid down in a desert 250 million years ago, have been shipped all over the country. Hopeman sandstone was used for the external cladding of the new extension to the National Museum of Scotland in Chambers Street, Edinburgh. It was also used in the approaches to the Forth Road Bridge, restorations at Cambridge University and many hydroelectric schemes. The quarry ceased production in 1996, but the Tennants company reopened it in 2011. When quarrying is not in progress it is possible to take the left fork and descend to the bottom of the quarry where you can see the remains of a harbour from which the stone was shipped, and also survey the huge extent of the cliff face with its subtle

Clashach Quarry.

gradations of honey-gold colour from one end of the cliff wall to the other.

Return to the path above the quarry. In May and June this leads through high gorse bushes ablaze with yellow. The next feature you come across is a somewhat weatherbeaten wooden fulmar which overlooks Primrose Bay, where, as the name implies, in spring primroses cascade down the grassy cliff faces in huge numbers.

The next object of interest is . . .

The Coastguard Lookout Tower

The broad path leading to this from the B9040 comes in a straight line from Gordonstoun House, which can be glimpsed from the top of the hill. In school term time a team from Gordonstoun use it as a base for coastal search and rescue practice, backing up the national Coastguard service whose Moray base is at Buckie. The tower, which is owned by Gordonstoun, was designed by Sir Martyn Beckett and was opened by the Duke of Edinburgh on 24 September 1955, replacing an earlier wooden hut erected in 1936 shortly after Gordonstoun itself was founded in 1934. There are three floors, the lowest houses the

The Coastguard Tower and Gordonstoun boys (1936).

The Coastguard Tower as it is today.

sleeping quarters; above this is a living area; and above this a lookout room and open gallery. There is currently no water or electricity supply.

Immediately below the tower, and facing seaward, lies . . .

The Sculptor's Cave

This cave, the largest of several such caves in the area, was cut into the Permian sandstone between Hopeman and Lossiemouth some 250 million years ago. Following a succession of Ice Ages in the last two million years, culminating in the last thaw round about 10,000 BC, the floor level has varied over centuries as sea levels have risen and fallen, and although the cave is now on a bank high above the tide level, the earlier sea levels can readily be traced on its walls. Much more remarkable, though, are the Pictish carvings on the one hand, and on the other the archaeological evidence which has come to light through the excavations which have continued there since the early years of the twentieth century. Approximately 2,000 human bones have been collected in the cave, varying in date from the late Bronze Age, say

1000-800 BC, through to the later Iron Age when Roman and Romano-British artefacts of comparable age to those found at Birnie were discovered, and more recently at Clarkly Hill near Burghead. Although the archaeological finds suggest that the cave was used as a dwelling, there is nothing to show that the people who lived there had a sea-based diet. However, the bones show compelling evidence that brutal practices such as decapitation must have occurred. Around 230 coins have also been found in the cave, only nine of which are Roman, the remainder probably dating from the pre-Pictish era of the fourth century. Modern archaeological interest was spurred by the findings of a doughty locally born lady, Miss Sylvia Benton (1887–1985) who, on visiting the cave in 1929, reported the floor to be 'strewn with human bones'. Many of these are now in the National Museum of Scotland in Edinburgh. The cave itself is now a Scheduled Monument Site in the care of Historic Environment Scotland. It was extensively excavated in 1979 by the county archaeologist Ian Shepherd and his wife, and explorations of the cave, in which archaeologists have abseiled down or used ladders, are now effectively complete. The cave can be accessed at low tide either from Primrose Bay or by walking on the rocks from east of the Coastguard station, but the going is very rough and this is not a recommended excursion.

A recently constructed path heads eastward from the Coastguard Tower and then on the landward side lies Covesea Links, an adventurous 9-hole golf course. Next comes . . .

Covesea Skerries Lighthouse

This part of the coastline, with its partially submerged rocky outcrops, has always been hazardous for shipping. Following a storm in the Moray Firth in November 1826 when sixteen vessels were sunk, plans were made for lighthouses at Tarbat Ness on the other side of the Firth, and here at Covesea, as well as a 12 metres tall cast-iron beacon tower which can still be seen on the Halliman

Covesea Skerries Lighthouse.

Skerries today. (The Covesea Skerries are a smaller unlit rock a little to the west.) The Covesea Skerries Lighthouse, designed by Alan Stevenson, was completed in 1846, and the tower on the Skerries was erected a year earlier.

Alan Stevenson was a member of the famous 'Lighthouse Stevensons' family who over a period of 150 years built most of the lighthouses around Scotland's coast. The building work was carried out by James Smith from Inverness. The lighthouse is 118 feet (36 metres) tall and its light had a range of 24 nautical miles. The lighthouse complex included the two keepers' cottages, now rented out as self-catering holiday lets. Covesea Skerries Lighthouse was automated in 1984. Its original Fresnel lens is now in the Lossiemouth Fisheries and Communities Museum on Pitgaveny Quay. The light was finally extinguished in 2012, after 166 years of service.

The lighthouse is now owned by the Covesea Lighthouse Community Company, which was formed by the local Business Association. Following a major grant from the Scottish Land Fund they were able to purchase the entire complex under the terms of the Land Reform (Scotland) Act 2003. The views from the lighthouse cover both sides of the Moray Firth as well as the RAF Lossiemouth air base. The lighthouse itself is open for tours on Saturdays from April until the end of October. These are run by volunteers, and require a minimum of 48 hours notice by calling 01343 810664 (if unanswered, leave a call-back message). Alternatively email *info@covesealighthouse.co.uk*.

Just east of the lighthouse is the Silver Sands caravan site and holiday complex, beyond which lies RAF Lossiemouth, one of the key elements in Britain's and NATO's defences.

Lossiemouth airfield was constructed in 1939 and was a major resource of Bomber Command during the Second World War. In 1946 it was handed over to the Fleet Air Arm as a Royal Naval Air Station known as *HMS Fulmar*. It was returned to the RAF in 1972. Today look out for Boeing Poseidon patrol aircraft taking off, successors to the former Buccaneer, Tornado and Typhoon fleets which once operated from the airfield.

Proceeding eastwards along the beach the path borders the Moray Golf Club, one of the most prestigious courses in the region where you can expect to pay around £100 for a round on the old course, about half of that on the new. In autumn sea buckthorn is conspicuous with its bright orange berries. At the end of the east beach is a boat-shaped monument to the Stotfield disaster, when on Christmas Day 1806 almost every single able-bodied male in the village perished in a huge storm. Stotfield is the most westerly of the three villages which as they expanded joined up to become the town of Lossiemouth. The others were Branderburgh and Seatown.

Lossiemouth

As with all the towns on the Way, although there is a designated waymarked route for the Moray Coast Trail, many visitors choose alternative routes, eventually rejoining the 'official' path at the other end of town.

The townward deviation from the route leads through the broad main street of Branderburgh heading to an elegant civic square where you have the choice of going up towards Prospect Terrace, or down towards the harbour.

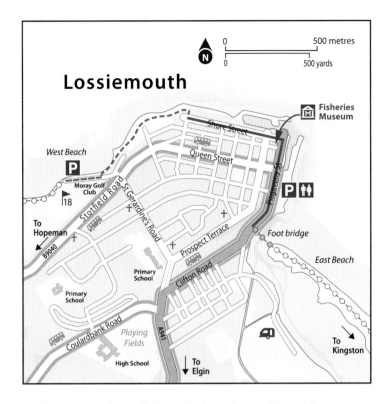

Lossiemouth and Branderburgh combined became a police burgh in 1890 under the name of Lossiemouth. From Prospect Terrace, the street which runs along the edge of the cliff on which the town is built, there is a view eastwards which Ramsay MacDonald described as the finest in the world — but then he was biased, as Lossiemouth is where he was born and spent much of his early life!

To the south the low-lying area looking south towards Elgin was once an arm of the sea, so that what is now Lossiemouth sat on an island, and ships sailed up to the foot of Spynie Palace. One of the two churches on the Terrace is named after Saint Gerardine, who according to legend walked the headland with a lantern to warn seafarers away from the dangerous Covesea and Halliman Skerries. The church, designed by Sir John James Burnet, was opened in 1901 and is notable for its Norman Romanesque tower, barrel-vaulted ceiling and some fine

Prospect Terrace, Lossiemouth.

stained glass. The other church, St James, was originally a Free Church whose foundation stone was laid in 1887. This church was destroyed by fire in 1932 and rebuilt the following year.

Lossiemouth, in honouring its most illustrious past resident, has a Ramsay MacDonald Trail which, if you follow it, will guide you to both of the above alternative routes. Unsurprisingly it passes the house in Moray Street which the future Prime Minister built for his young family in 1908. He had originally planned to build his house on Prospect Terrace, however the then town council were not prepared to have such a prestigious site marred by the home of a 'rabid pacifist' and Ramsay had to settle for The Hillocks in Moray Street in the lower part of the town. The Hillocks has a plaque, but is privately owned and still in the hands of his descendants. It is worth pausing here to consider how, when Parliament was in recess in the early 1930s, UK government business was conducted from this spot.

Lossiemouth Harbour

In 1685, Elgin burgh council called upon a German engineer, Peter Brauss, to look at the viability of building a harbour at the mouth of the River Lossie to compete with those of Findhorn and Garmouth. He decided that a harbour could indeed be established. The first efforts at the beginning of the eighteenth century seem to have failed, but by 1764 the new jetty had been built at a cost of £1,200.

At the time that the new river-mouth harbour was being constructed, so too was Branderburgh with its characteristic wide streets forming a planned development on a rectangular grid. The builders, craftsmen and merchants occupied the grand new houses, while the fishermen occupied the more lowly houses at Seatown. Later, a canal with a sluice visible to the south was designed by Thomas Telford to drain Loch Spynie. This was constructed between 1805 and 1810 and entered the River Lossie in this area, thereby creating a physical barrier between the two communities which is still clearly visible.

By the early nineteenth century, the river harbour was busy but this was unsustainable in the long term. This meant that an alternative solution was sought. In 1834, the Stotfield and Lossiemouth Harbour Company was formed to look into building a new harbour at Stotfield Point.

The construction of the new harbour was carried out between 1837 and 1839, though initially in a relatively small way after a ceremony in which the first stone was laid by the local laird Colonel Brander of Pitgaveny, one of the large inland estates. This was the beginning of the final phase of building what was to become Branderburgh. However, by 1858, the basin had been enlarged further and deepened to 4.9 metres at spring tides. This encouraged many fishing families from up and down the coast to move to the town.

Above, Lossiemouth Harbour in 1966; below, as it is today.

The harbour, as well as now having a large herring fleet, also shared the available space with trading ships. This prompted the now renamed Elgin and Lossiemouth Harbour Company to build a second basin at a cost of £18,000. This basin was intended solely for fishing boats and opened in 1860. A century later, fishing boats still dominated the harbour, which is now largely a pleasure marina with tall modern flats to match.

Nowadays the quayside with its converted warehouses, one of them the Fisheries Museum run by volunteers, has more of the atmosphere of a continental resort.

The routes through Lossiemouth converge at Seatown, a complex of low-lying fishermen's houses established at the end of the seventeenth century to replace the old port at Spynie which had become landlocked. When the new harbour servicing larger trading vessels at the river mouth was built, the fishermen did not use the new pier, but continued to sail their boats up to the beach at Seatown. Seatown is called 'The Toonie' by its inhabitants and sometimes referred to as the 'Dogwall', a reference to dog-skins that once were dried here before being turned into floats for nets.

The opening of the Morayshire Railway persuaded Colonel Brander to build a footbridge from Seatown to the east beach to encourage more day visitors in the summer months. The replacement for that bridge was built by the now defunct Elgin Harbour Board and carried the Moray Way to the east bank of the Lossie. It survived until it was condemned as unsafe in 2020 and has now been replaced with a bridge further downstream.

River Lossie Estuary

Huge flocks of wintering wigeon are regularly to be seen here, and flocks of snow buntings are also fairly frequent in the winter months, flitting swiftly over the dunes. Sanderling move back and forth along the water's edge, racing along on their short legs as if propelled by clockwork. Crested tits may be sighted in the Lossie Forest which lies beyond the east beach, but are difficult to spot unless you chance on a feeding station topped up by local bird enthusiasts. Crossbills are only seen in irruptions, so that most of the time they are not present, but when they are (usually in late winter or early spring), they will be everywhere!

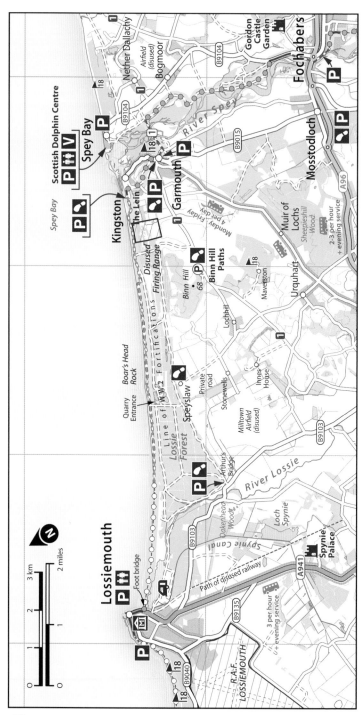

Moray Coast Trail east, Lossiemouth to Spey Bay.

Lossiemouth to the Track Junction at NJ269685

To continue on the Moray Way from Lossiemouth, cross the newly-constructed bridge from the esplanade and head along the shore with the dunes on your right.

Although no longer surviving, there were pillboxes and a line of anti-tank cubes here covering access from the mouth of the river into the town. Surprisingly the dunes closer to Lossiemouth are not an entirely natural feature, since they were created in the 1900s in a scheme to protect Seatown from storms, which involved dumping old railway carriages and allowing sand to blow over them.

After a while the sand underfoot gives way to shingle, where eventually regenerating pine seedlings give a foretaste of the Lossie Forest which you are approaching. After 2½ miles you will reach a signpost at NJ269685 where the beach route and forest route described below converge.

Alternative Route Taking in Second World War Defences

After crossing the footbridge (see p. 61), walk south of the dunes until you reach a broad area of coastal grassland frequently abundant in birdlife. (At high tides you will have to skirt the edge of the dunes rather uncomfortably.) After rounding this marshy area you will come to a point where a firmer footpath takes over, becoming a broader forest track, and then a major forestry road. Continue along this until you come to a junction where there are anti-tank cubes on both sides of the road. Take time to make a detour and follow the line westwards through the woods. Here you will come to a pillbox which was probably heavily camouflaged when built, but is now even further overgrown. Climb the bank alongside to get a view of the algae-lined basin of the Innes Canal, which would have been a formidable obstacle for tanks. When you return to the road junction a waymarker points the way westwards alongside the line of cubes between the trees, until it reaches a large pillbox on a hillock where the line of cubes turns towards the sea and the path reaches the fingerpost at NJ269685 previously noted.

Cycling can be recommended if the aim is to see as much of the Second World War defences as possible. In this case, rather than struggling with the early stages of the above route alongside the dunes, a better plan is to start at the Lossie Forest car park near Arthur's Bridge, and follow major roads towards the road junction at the line of cubes at NJ263686. The tracks through the Lossie Forest are excellent terrain for mountain-bikes, with well-surfaced and almost level forestry roads. A cluster of eight pillboxes at one time bordered the canal. One has been mentioned above, another is at NJ255681, others may be buried in the forest.

Second World War Defences from Fingerpost to Kingston

Carry on for about 500 yards east of the fingerpost, and you come to a line of anti-tank cubes with pillboxes at about quarter mile intervals. Here you start the six-mile trek to Kingston, which is notable for having the longest and best preserved stretch of anti-invasion cubes and pillboxes in Scotland.

The section of beach between Lossiemouth and Kingston was on the list of UK beaches deemed vulnerable to invasion in 1940 and 1941. (Hitler had nominated 2 July 1940 as the date for the invasion of Britain — not an anniversary that is much celebrated!) There were two airfields behind the beach, Milltown, which was a satellite of Lossiemouth, and also a civilian airfield about which little is known, at Lunan Wood, about two miles up the Spey from its mouth.

The stretch of beach with military remains has been given the curious nickname of 'the Unknown'. Walking along it is akin to being in an open-air museum commemorating the time, not so long ago, when the whole region

A searchlight post at Innes Links.

was a war-zone, in which frenetic effort was expended on the construction of anti-tank cubes and pillboxes. These, with their machine-gun shelves, would then have com- manded wide views of the Moray Firth. Now they look out uselessly on the vast shingle banks which have built up in the intervening years. They compare strikingly with the defences at Burghead where the effect of wind and water has submerged both cubes and pillboxes under sand and caused both to tilt at crazy angles. At Innes Links, just behind the line of cubes, there are two well-preserved gunhouses, screened off by metal barriers with 'Danger- ous Buildings' notices. One of the gunhouses, opening out like a huge open-air stage, hosts the work of local graffiti artists – a temple of World War!

Two searchlight houses flank the gunhouses, and in- land there are the remains of an accommodation block, ammunition stores and engine houses.

The contract for constructing the battery was signed in April 1941. In October 1940 the defence of the beach from Covesea to Kingston was assigned to three companies of the 12th Cameronians. They were replaced in early 1941 by units of Pioneer companies who were stationed

*A pillbox and line of cubes with the Moray Coast Trail
on the right.*

there and took over the coastal defences from Findhorn
to Kingston, assisted by the Home Guard.

The Moray coastal defences were described by Bar-
tlam and Keillar in a reasonably comprehensive book
World War Two in Moray (2003), although there is a fuller
picture in Henry Wills' *Pillboxes: A Study of the UK Defences 1940* (1985), cataloguing every pillbox in the UK.
Gordon Barclay in *If Hitler Comes* (2013) gives a detailed
account of defence preparations throughout Scotland. An
unintended consequence of this wartime construction is
that pillboxes in general make good winter shelters for
insects which spend the winter as adults, such as peacock
butterflies.

The Moray pillboxes and anti-tank obstacles were
constructed at high speed, but rather later than the
main deployment of them in England, and only when
the vulnerability of the Moray coast beaches to German
invasion came to be appreciated following the German
occupation of Norway in the summer of 1940. In the
UK about 18,000 pillboxes were built during 1940 of
which roughly twenty per cent were still extant in 2003.
Burghead Bay had nine in total, most of which are tilted
randomly into the sea. There are twenty-two on the coast

between Lossiemouth and Kingston, and also a well-camouflaged one in the woods about two miles east of Lossiemouth, beside a long line of tank-traps running between the trees. Pillboxes were constructed from a mixture of brick, stone and breeze concrete. There was another small group of pillboxes in the Craigellachie/ Dufftown area, one of them right on the Speyside Way at Craigellachie, on a spot where Scottish Water now have a building.

Remains of the Moray coastal defences: above, an accommodation block; below, an ammunition store.

An overgrown pillbox.

By early 1942 pillboxes were deemed redundant, and by the end of 1943 they became officially surplus to requirements – in plain terms, useless – after Bletchley Park codebreakers discovered that Hitler had called off his invasion plans. The sea surged in relentlessly, piling up shingle in front of parts of the defensive line and burying others.

Bin Hill

Before the route reaches Kingston there are a few signposted trails through the bracken leading to this modest summit, which is nevertheless a good viewpoint – a worthwhile detour if time allows. The military rifle and firing ranges shown on OS maps to the west of Kingston were decommissioned in 2019, and the Ministry of Defence have embarked on a project to clear and decontaminate the area.

As the trail nears Kingston it crosses an area called the Lein, once the site of a concrete fabrication yard, now an area predominantly of gorse and grass officially protected as a local nature reserve, on account of the presence of rare alpine-type plants which grow there and on the shingle.

There is evidence that many centuries ago the Spey turned westward from its present course and entered the sea via the Lein. More recently Kingston had its moment of fame on 23 June 1650, when somewhere along the shore the 20-year-old Charles II, returning from exile in Holland on his way to be crowned King of Scotland at Scone in 1651, was carried ashore on the shoulders of Thomas Milne, one of the brawny local fishermen. This may be where the name Kingston, 'King's town', came from.

Kingston

This quiet settlement today contrasts greatly with the bustle of industry which characterised it in the eighteenth century. If in 1710 you had been on the banks of the Spey at Garmouth, you might have seen a celebration following the arrival of the first pine log that had been floated all the way down the Spey from Nethybridge. This successful trial was developed on an industrial scale and led to the opening in 1786 of a shipbuilding yard at Kingston which was to continue until the 1850s. When the Spey spates were due, rafts of logs were floated down the river from the Abernethy forest, where a network of Highland burns facilitated the collection of timber into a gathering point on the Spey. Here logs were sorted and stamped with the owner's initials and then floated down, either individually or loosely tied together and accompanied by men in *currachs*, coracle-like boats ridden by two 'floaters' with 'cleeks', poles with iron-pointed heads for manoeuvring the rafts of logs. Later, rafts were constructed fastened together with wire loops, and at the peak of the trade giant convoys of up to 30,000 logs were floated down, operated by up to 80 men. Only a small proportion of the floated timber was retained to make boats, the majority was exported. The floaters also took advantage of the opportunity to make money by acting as ferrymen for goods and people as they sailed down the river, a journey which from Nethybridge to Garmouth took about 12 hours. These early foresters and raft drivers were seasonal workers, typically crofters for

The Browlands Stones.

whom the wages from the timber work assured payment of rents to the laird for the rest of the year.

An alternative derivation for the name Kingston is that it dates from 1784, when two entrepreneurs from Kingston-upon-Hull established a timber business there, which involved constructing a canal to make it easier to launch boats from the shipyard into the river. The Kingston boatyard was a hive of activity in the late eighteenth century. According to the *Statistical Account* of 1793, there were twenty-three wooden ships built between 1785 and 1792 with an average weight of around 200 tons and masts up to 60 feet tall. There was also a repair yard. The largest vessel, *The Duke of Gordon*, weighed in at 500 tons.

Timber was not the only the only source of maritime traffic. There were over a hundred sailings a year exporting, in addition to timber, salmon, yarn, oats and meal, and importing coal (much of it from Sunderland), salt, iron, empty kits (lidded wooden containers) and miscellaneous household goods.

Proceeding from Kingston to Garmouth you can walk down the road, but a better alternative is an excellent gently rising inland path starting from a footbridge at

NJ337654 and continuing via School Brae to the central car park at Garmouth. This car park is a good entry/exit point for walking the Moray Way one section at a time. Near the summit of the little hill a fingerpost directs you to the Browlands Stones. These form a small circle and are believed to mark a prehistoric site dating from around 1500 BC. To view these it is easier just to go straight ahead and then, just as you finally descend to the village, look for a fence post and a path on the right which takes you to both the stones and the nineteenth-century water tower which used to serve both villages.

Garmouth

Garmouth (possibly Gaelic *geàrr magh* = narrow plain, referring to the flat ground between the water tower hill and the flat area on which the golf course lies) is both the larger and older neighbour of Kingston, whose eighteenth-century prosperity came about through its being an agricultural, mercantile and industrial centre, as well as a major port of Moray well into the nineteenth century. At that time Duncan's iron foundry was one of the leading employers in the town.

A Garmouth street.

71

The former Garmouth Free Church.

Like its younger neighbour Fochabers, Garmouth was a Burgh of Barony in the eighteenth century. Today it is a quiet country town whose population, with Kingston included, is around 650. The narrow twisting streets at its centre are more reminiscent of an English country village than a former Scottish industrial hub. The distinctive church tower belonged to what was a United Free church prior to its union with the established Church of Scotland in 1929. What was then the established Church's building became in time the village hall. The present Church of Scotland building lies inland at Speymouth between Garmouth and Masstodloch – called the Red Church because of the rich colour of its sandstone. In the late twentieth century the Reverend Alexander Macaulay was the last serving Church of Scotland minister who actively farmed his glebe, the land attached to the church and used in the past for agriculture and grazing. It is said that he planted his own barley to ensure that the crop would not end up supplying a distillery!

The earliest recorded mention of Garmouth is in a deed of 1237, and by 1393 it had received a charter to become a trading port for Elgin, superseding the one at Spynie (see p. 61) which had silted up. Until the construction of Lossiemouth Harbour, Garmouth and Findhorn competed as the Moray's two harbours for exports and imports. A charter of 1587 established Garmouth as a Burgh of Barony, entitling it to have a local court, a mercat cross and annual fairs, of which one, the Maggie Fair, continued to be celebrated on the last Saturday in June, until Covid. The original timber pier was built in the seventeenth century, but the harbour was never any more than a tidal basin from which big ships either beached on the shore at high tide or used smaller boats to unload cargo and passengers.

In the late eighteenth century Garmouth had a large sawmill which supported the shipbuilding industry at Kingston, which employed twenty-eight ships' carpenters and almost as many millers. The timber was said to give great satisfaction to its customers, so that it was expected that the trade would continue and increase. In terms of mercantile traffic through the port in the year 1792 there were 109 outward sailings, mostly exporting timber, but also boiled salmon bound for London as at Findhorn, and 23 inward sailings, about half of which had a cargo of coal, then a luxury item.

Garmouth Station

At one time the line was double-tracked, but it was soon singled. The station had a wooden building with two platforms, similar to others on the coastal route. A signal box and two sidings lay at the eastern end. Apart from a short closure for renovation work in 1928, the line to Garmouth remained in use until the Beeching cuts in 1965, when the coastal rail route was closed, bringing yet another era in the town's history to an end. Today all that is left are names — Station Road, also the small housing estate appropriately called The Sidings, and the Whistlestop Pond on the south side of the old line, memorials to the days when steam engines with their carriages puffed through Garmouth.

Garmouth Railway Viaduct

Garmouth Viaduct was opened in 1886 by the Great North of Scotland Railway (GNoSR). The engineers were Blaikie Bros., Aberdeen. The great length of the main span was necessitated by the constantly wandering course of the Spey near its mouth.

In 1883 plans were announced by GNoSR to build a coastal railway passing through Garmouth. However, the GNoSR engineers faced a problem before building could commence. With no rock banks north of the Fochabers road bridge, they decided to sink paired cast-iron cylinders 14 feet in diameter, filled with concrete and sunk to a depth of 52 feet below the level of the riverbed. Metal blocks with a total weight of 150 tons were placed round the inside of the cylinders. With pumps working continually to keep

The Garmouth Viaduct.

the insides free of water, men descended inside and carefully dismantled the base of each cylinder, allowing it to sink further into the bed.

At the time it was built and for many years to follow, the 350 ft (106 m) central span remained the longest on any single-line bridge in Scotland and the second largest in the UK, exceeded only by Brunel's Britannia Bridge across the Menai Straits. The three spans on either side are each 100 ft (30 m) long, giving a total length of 947 ft (288 m). The outer spans have level girders 10 ft (3 m) high and the centre has a bowstring 40 ft 8 in (12 m) in height.

A civil engineer called Fyfe, from Aberdeen, was the contractor with the difficult task of forming the foundations, erecting the piers, and diverting the river's flow while work progressed. Messrs. Blaikie of Aberdeen constructed the metal bridgework. The *Elgin Courant*, always up-to-date with current news, describes the completed work as 'if not the prettiest, one of the most durable and substantial bridges in the kingdom.'

Although completion took only three years, work did not always run smoothly. From 1883 to 1885, as construction progressed, spring thaws played havoc with the diverted river on several occasions, halting work until it was established in its new channel. Dykes on the embankment had to be strengthened and in November 1885 a new problem arose when the navvies demanded a pay rise of a penny per hour for their work of diverting the river. When this was refused, 300 of them marched in a body through the streets of Garmouth in a belligerent manner to the new station, found the timekeeper and seriously assaulted him. An all-round brawl followed with several men being injured. Eventually 130 men recommenced the work at the original rate of pay.

By January of 1886 the bridge was nearing completion, but the Duke of Richmond and Gordon was not pleased. He was convinced the main flow of the river would not be reinstated before the commencement of the salmon fishing season on 1 May, and lodged a claim for compensation of £21,000. This legal battle was not resolved until

December 1889 when the action was finally dismissed by Lord Kinnear.

In March 1886, prior to the official opening of the bridge, tests were run to assess its strength. A testing load of 400 tons, with the GNoSR's heaviest engines pulling twenty trucks of gravel, deflected the central span by only one and one-eighth of an inch. The Spey was now redirected into its new central channel beneath the middle span, but the following winter it broke through the new gravel embankments and returned to its old eastern channel. As a consequence you do not pass the main part of the river until you are almost over the bridge itself.

In April 1886 the first train chugged through Garmouth on the coastal route. However, as with many wonderful innovations, there was a downside. The dying shipping industry, once thriving on the Kingston shoreline, was dealt a death blow with much of the imported and exported freight now being carried by rail.

For a short while in 1972 there was talk of turning the viaduct into a road bridge to ease traffic on the A96, giving a more direct route to Buckie. The cost at that time was estimated at £100,000, with British Rail offering to sell the bridge for £5,000. However, it was decided the idea was too costly and impractical, and so it was left to serve as a public walkway with maintenance by Moray Council at that time costing £700 a year.

After crossing the viaduct you turn right and switch from the Moray Coast Trail to the Speyside Way. Before doing so, consider turning left and taking a detour northwards to reach the mouth of the river, where you will find the . . .

Whale and Dolphin Conservation Society Centre and Tugnet Ice House at Spey Bay

This is clearly a good spot from which to snatch a glimpse of dolphins, since every time anyone spots one, a bell is rung so that everyone can spill out from the café to see it! In summer it is possible to get sightings of ospreys, as well as divers and many other sea birds. Bird lists are maintained which guarantee daily updated information about the latest sightings. For those interested in botany the centre lies close to one of the most notable stretches of shingle bank in Britain, with many unusual plants.

The Ice House, the largest building of its type in the UK,dates from 1830. It is A-listed and is run by the charity Whale and Dolphin Conservation as an information centre. It contains much of interest and is well worth a visit. For opening hours call 01249 449500 or visit *www.dolphincentre. whales.org*. The capacious Ice House is testimony to the thriving trade that from the eighteenth century benefited from the Spey. Like the Findhorn (see p. 34) the Spey was awash with salmon which were sent by the many thousands in kits to London fishmongers, who probably had financial investments in the trade. The salmon employed significant numbers of men using eight-man crews in 'cobles' in much the same way as at Findhorn.

There were also fish traps (cruives) set in the river which restricted the passage of many of the salmon beyond the lower reaches of the river. The Duke of Gordon owned seven-ninths of the fishery itself and the Earl of Moray two-ninths. When the London market was satiated by fresh fish, the salmon were salted and sold on the continent. So great was this trade by the end of the century that there was little salmon left by the end of the season to supply local demand.

Extension to Buckie

To continue along the Moray Way you must return to the path junction east of the viaduct. However if you wish to pursue the Speyside Way to its final destination in Buckie, continue eastwards for a further six miles. At first Spey Bay Golf Course lies to the north, of which Ramsay MacDonald was an enthusiastic patron when parliamentary duties allowed. The large building in the background of the photograph overleaf of Ramsay MacDonald golfing is the former Richmond and Gordon Hotel, opened as a

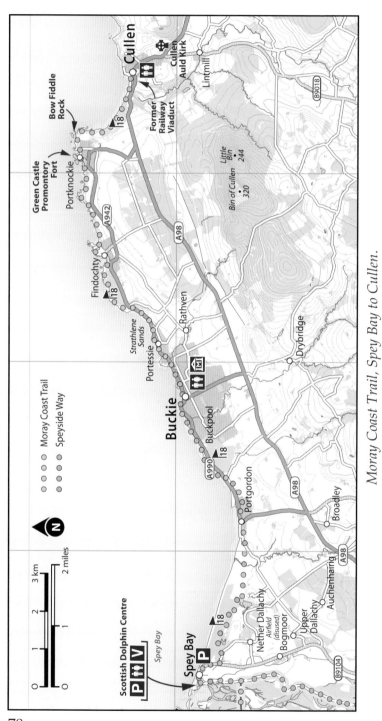

Moray Coast Trail, Spey Bay to Cullen.

Cullen

Cullen
Auld Kirk

Lintmill

B9018

Bow Fiddle
Rock

18

Former
Railway
Viaduct

Green Castle
Promontory
Fort

Portknockie

Little
Bin
244

Bin of Cullen
320

A942

A98

Findochty

18

Strathlene
Sands

Rathven

Portessie

Drybridge

Buckie

Buckpool

18

Moray Coast Trail

Speyside Way

A990

Portgordon

A98

Broadley

N

Auchenhairig

A98

3 km

2

1

2 miles

1

Nether Dallachy

Bogmoor

Airfield
(disused)

Upper
Dallachy

B9104

Scottish Dolphin Centre

Spey Bay

P

Spey Bay

P

18

1

0

0

Ramsay MacDonald golfing at Spey Bay.

favoured destination for the wealthy when golfing took off as a leisure pursuit. In the First World War it was turned into an officers' convalescent home, and in the Second World War it became quarters for RAF personnel at the nearby Dallachy air station. It burnt down in 1965 to be replaced by the Spey Bay Hotel. This closed in 2006 and was later demolished.

There is a slight divergence of the routes around Port Gordon, where the Speyside Way follows the coastline while the Moray Coast Trail goes higher giving views over the rooftops.

The climax of this stretch of the Moray Coast Trail is the final two miles between Portknockie and Cullen where, after emerging from a cutting, the line proceeds on a high embankment sweeping over the rooftops of Cullen on bridges which the Great North of Scotland Railway was obliged to build at great expense to avoid encroaching on the Earl of Seafield's land.

2
THE SPEYSIDE WAY

It would be wrong to interpret 'Speyside' as meaning 'along the banks of the Spey', since for much of its course the Speyside Way lies far from the river's banks. Instead 'Speyside' should be seen as a name for a region encompassing wide swathes of land on each side of the river.

From the path junction between the Moray Coast Trail and the Speyside Way, the latter is routed parallel to the river, but at at a little distance from it and through woods. It is worth taking one of the side paths to view the sandbanks which river action has thrown up on the west side.

The surrounding area is notable for the red colour of the stone outcrops and buildings. Eons ago the sea levels were higher than now, and it is no accident that the settlement viewed to the west in the distance is called Bogmoor. The first settlement to be encountered in the Moray Way circuit is . . .

Fochabers

With a population of around 2,600, Fochabers is somewhere between a town and a village. It was laid out in 1776 by Alexander Gordon, 4th Duke of Gordon, as one of several villages created during the Scottish Enlightenment. Like many others, for example Grantown-on-Spey founded in the same year, it has straight, wide streets in a rectangular layout based on a central square. It is not cynical to say that the site of of both planned villages was chosen to keep the crofters, weavers and shopkeepers at an appropriate distance from the grandeur of the castle surroundings. Technically Fochabers was a Burgh of Barony, with a Baron Bailie appointed from among the gentry to dispense local justice. The name Fochabers

Opposite: Walkers at Knockfrink Hill on the Speyside Way.

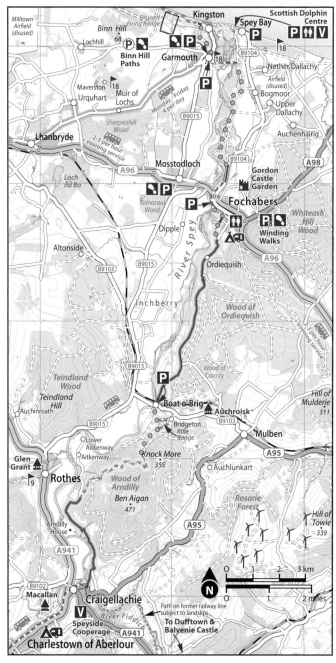

Speyside Way, Spey Bay to Craigellachie.

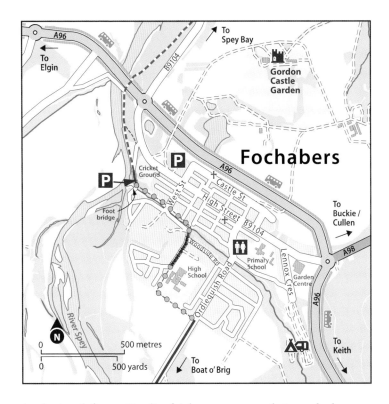

is derived from Gaelic *faich* = a green plot, and *aber* = a junction of two waters. The Gaelic tongue survived locally until the early eighteenth century, although by the time of the *Statistical Account* at the end of the century it had completely died out as spoken speech in this area.

The Bellie Kirk (Gaelic *beul-aith* = the mouth of the ford) in the square is of architectural interest, as is the Gothic Revival Gordon Chapel, first opened in 1836, which contains the largest collection of pre-Raphaelite stained glass in Scotland. This was partly financed by the sale of some of the Duchess's jewellery. The interior was reconstructed in 1874, and in 1935 ownership passed from the Duke of Gordon to the Crown.

Bellie is also the name of the ancient parish in which Fochabers lies. The Gaelic name, 'mouth of the ford' reflects the fact that the silt and debris of the floods of 1768 closed off an inlet of the river just upstream from

The Gordon Chapel.

the church, which in 1746 had provided an excellent entry point for the Duke of Cumberland. He led his army over the ford en route to what proved to be the Battle of Culloden. The present bridges over the Spey replaced a ferry known as 'the boat of Bog', this name deriving from Gaelic *bogra-gbdhu* = windy bog, from the strong west and north winds which characterise the area.

Between 1893 and 1966 Fochabers had a railway station called Fochabers Town on the west bank of the Spey (see p. 192), although after 1931 this was open only to freight. This continued until the 1960s, albeit with only one train a day.

The most noted tourist attraction in Fochabers is the castle's walled garden, approached by a prominent entrance gateway over a little bridge at the west end of the village. Be aware that the drive is long, but it is a significant and worthwhile deviation from the Moray Way when passing through Fochabers.

Gordon Castle, Fochabers

The castle, which in the weeks leading up to Culloden was headquarters to both the Hanoverian and Jacobite forces, is not open to the public but its walled garden is;

the final restoration of the garden was completed in 2022. Gordon Castle was extensively rebuilt by the 4th Duke of Gordon in 1770 when the garden was first started. It covers almost eight acres and is one of the largest and, at over 200 years old, one of the oldest kitchen gardens in Britain. It has been lovingly redesigned to be both beautiful and productive, containing, it is said, 259 espaliered fruit trees! The highly popular restaurant and visitor centre were opened in the garden in 2014. The garden itself (admission at the time of writing is £7) and restaurant are open all the year round (though in 2021 from Wednesday to Sunday only), and the garden shop sells an extensive range of produce.

Fochabers Bridges

The Speyside Way passes under two bridges crossing the Spey; the first carries the A96, the second, upstream, is

Gordon Castle Gardens from the air (photo by Ed Bollom).

Fochabers Old Bridge, now accessible only to pedestrians and cyclists. The factory complex of the Baxters company, world-famous for their soups and other food products, lies on the west bank just north of the first bridge. Baxters started from simple beginnings in 1868 when George Baxter, a young gardener, opened a grocery shop in Fochabers selling his wife's products. Soup production started in 1929 and in the Second World War the company kept going by supplying jam to the forces. In the twenty-first century Baxters has expanded with takeovers to become a large multinational multi-brand company, while retaining central control within the Baxter family. Until 2019 there was an extensive visitor centre and Highland village at the site, but sadly this is now permanently closed.

The original Spey Bridge at Fochabers opened in 1804, replacing a ferry. Earlier in 1746 the Duke of Cumberland's army, marching from Aberdeen to victory at Culloden, waded across unopposed by the Jacobites. Much of the 1804 bridge was swept away in the great Moray floods of August 1829, to be partly replaced in 1832 by a wooden arch. Telford offered a plan for a suspension bridge, but this was rejected as too expensive, and the 1832 bridge

The road and rail bridges at Boat o' Brig.

survived until dry rot forced a rebuild in 1854. The latter is the bridge you see today.

From Fochabers the Moray Way proceeds down West Street, then cuts through to Ordiequish Road which becomes a hilly minor public road leading past the car park for the Earth Pillars, curious red earth deposits laid down by glaciers centuries ago — these are worth a glance, although now rather overgrown. The Way then passes under the arch of a railway bridge to Boat o' Brig, where road and rail bridges cross the Spey in parallel. Until 1830 the Spey crossing here was by a ferry. A new chain bridge proposed by the local MP was in place until 1854 when the present road bridge was built. The rail bridge, paid for largely by the Inverness & Aberdeen Joint Railway so that the Elgin-Keith link could be connected, was completed in 1856.

After Boat o' Brig comes one of the longest parts of the Speyside Way without any motor road entry point. The path rises uphill towards Bridgeton, where it goes east, then does a U-turn to the right, passing the Speyside Gun Club range which is well signposted. Make sure you follow a waymarker where the rifle range drive heads off to the left, and the much less obvious Speyside Way becomes a grassy path.

The narrow path continues for a while along the level, before climbing uphill to meet a main forestry track at NJ 316496. (If you are doing this section from south to north, be sure to look out for this sudden transition in path type.) From here the path climbs, following wide forest tracks used by large heavy timber extraction lorries. It contours along the side of Ben Aigan, rising to a height of 280 m (950 ft) with occasional good views of the Spey valley below.

There is a signpost pointing to a viewpoint overlooking the steep ravine called the Red Sheugh. From here the descent to Craigellachie begins, with occasional glimpses of the town of Rothes in the distance, eventually coming to a gated entry to the Ben Aigan forest where the path joins a minor public road leading past the fine privately owned mansion house of Arndilly, whose grounds stretch

View looking north over the Red Sheugh.

down to the Spey. Arndilly is where Edward I is said to have forded the Spey in the course of his 1296 campaign against the Scots. It was once the seat of a cadet branch of the Clan Grant dynasty.

In Craigellachie it is well worth while to take a short detour from the track to cross the Spey at . . .

The Thomas Telford Bridge at Craigellachie

This bridge was opened in 1814, replacing an earlier bridge destroyed in a great spate in the nineteenth century. It is now open only to foot and cycle traffic, having been closed to vehicles when the new bridge over the A941 was constructed in 1972.

Thomas Telford, towards the end of a distinguished career as the leading civil engineer in the UK, designed the Craigellachie bridge in parallel with a similar one at Bonar Bridge, which did not survive the severe floods of 1892. The poet Southey described the approach to the latter as like seeing a spider's web in the air – 'the finest thing that was ever made by God or man!' Even the official report on the Craigellachie bridge eulogises it: 'the combination of the rock face of Moinian gneiss with the slender appearance of the iron arch, made more beautiful by not being in contact with the masonry arches, render this spot one of the most remarkable in Scotland.'

Perhaps even more remarkable is that the ironwork of the bridge was made, not in Scotland, but in Telford's favoured iron foundry at Plas Kynastin in Wales, from which the parts were conveyed by sea. The bridge took ten months to construct and opened in 1814.

A more human side to the bridge's story is that the agreed contract price for the bridge as estimated by Telford was £8,200. Although the contractors worked with great enthusiasm and speed, the surveyors had greatly underestimated the difficulty of the work, but refused to make

The Thomas Telford Bridge, Craigellachie.

any allowance for the consequent increases in costs, and this caused many of the local contractors to lose money, leading in some cases to great hardship and distress.

The name Craigellachie, from the Gaelic *Craig-Elachie*, 'Rock of Alarm', probably refers to the hill at the west end of the bridge, which presumably served as a signal station in olden times. There is a rock overlooking Aviemore which is also called Craigellachie.

Craigellachie Church

This relatively modest building which lies on the A941 road to Dufftown was opened in 1871 thanks to the generosity of Margaret Macpherson-Grant (see p. 95) who was a staunch Episcopalian and made it a condition that it should be used as a school during the week. This continued until 1901 when Craigellachie Primary School was opened, and the church passed into the hands of the Church of Scotland.

Other Diversions from Craigellachie

There are two diversions which might appeal to those without cars, as both have a regular public bus service. They are to the towns predominantly known for making whisky, namely Rothes and Dufftown (populations around 1,400 and 1,600 respectively). Another recommended diversion is to the Macallan Distillery visitor centre, opened in 2018, but this is not served by bus. The Rothes Way, a footpath following the old railway line from Craigellachie via Dandaleith, is in the process of being completed at the time of writing and offers good views of the Spey.

Rothes

Of Rothes Castle little remains except a single wall looking down over the High Street. The castle was probably founded in the twelfth century by the de Pollocs, one of the Norman families posted into Moray to subdue the

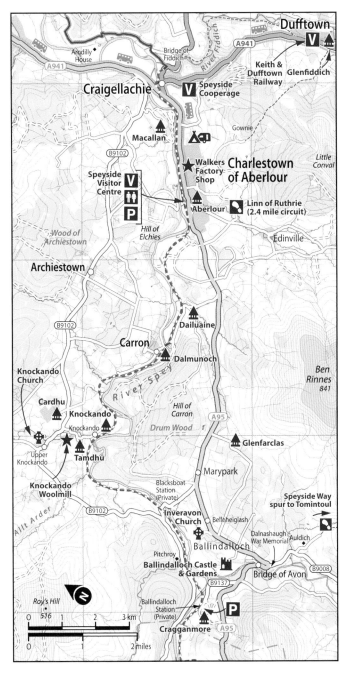

Speyside Way, Craigellachie to Ballindalloch.

rebellious population. Edward I stayed in the castle on the first of his raids into Moray in 1296. Alexander, the Wolf of Badenoch, was also a guest there in the fourteenth century. It later became the seat of the Leslie family who became Earls of Rothes in the fifteenth century. In 1662 it was torched by townsmen in the belief that thieves were being harboured there. After this the stones were pillaged for building houses in the town.

Rothes is home to four distilleries, Glen Rothes (Edrington Group), Glen Spey (Diageo), Speyburn (Inver House Distillers) and Glen Grant (Campari). Only the last of these has tours and a visitor centre. Its garden is unique among the Speyside distilleries and this alone makes a detour to Rothes worthwhile. Another feature of the town is the Dounie, a steep-sided glaciated valley with some spectacular outcrops (see p. 9). This can be approached by going up Burnside Road and continuing through the premises of Glen Rothes Distillery. Rothes parish church in the centre of the town is one of the oldest working village churches in Moray.

Dufftown

Dufftown can be reached from Craigellachie by a pleasant footpath which proceeds up Glen Fiddich along the track of the former Great North of Scotland Railway (see p. 189). The town was originally called Mortlach, a name which still survives in the name of its church. Founded in 1817, like Grantown and Fochabers it is another Speyside village established by the local landowner, in this case the Earl of Fife, in order to relieve local poverty and unemployment, brought about by soldiers returning from the Napoleonic wars. The town is attractively surrounded by hills. Its main thoroughfare, Balvenie Street, is wide and spacious and opens out to an iconic grey granite clock tower. Those well-versed in folk music may like to note that the notorious eighteenth-century fiddler and freebooter James MacPherson of 'MacPherson's Rant' fame was hanged here, and the clock was the one which the magistrates famously advanced a quarter of an hour, in case a reprieve came just before the appointed hour of execution! Dufftown has a greater concentration of distilleries in its locality than any other Speyside town or village; nine in total, of which three are disused. Mortlach Parish Church is a largely nineteenth-century building on one of the oldest sites of continuous worship in Scotland, having been founded around AD 560 by St Moluag, a contemporary of St Columba. The church-yard has a watchtower which was used to guard against nineteenth-century grave-robbers. Mortlach may have been the scene of a battle in 1010 when Malcolm II defeated the Danes (see also Sueno's Stone, p. 24).

On the western outskirts of the town Balvenie Castle is an impressive, much fought-over ruin, now in the care of Historic Environment Scotland. It did not open in 2021 because of the pandemic, but HES are currently working towards opening up sites like this again and those who want to visit should check the HES website, *www.historicenvironment.scot.*

Balvenie Castle

Built by the Comyns in the thirteenth century, Balvenie changed hands several times, first being occupied by the Douglas family in Robert the Bruce's time, then, follow-ing their downfall, passing to John Stewart, 1st Duke of Atholl, in 1460. The Stewart Earls of Atholl retained Bal-venie until the seventeenth century and were responsible for much of its handsome rebuilding. Its status as a lead-ing Scottish castle was such that Edward I stayed there in 1296 in the course of invading Scotland, while in 1562 Mary Queen of Scots stayed two nights in the course of her campaign against the Gordons. In 1644 the Marquis of Montrose sheltered there, using it as a base that was safe from the Marquis of Argyll's cavalry following the battle of Fyvie. It was a Government garrison at the time of the 1715 Jacobite rebellion, but three years later it was abandoned and passed to the Crown. Thereafter it was bought by the Duffs who became the Earls of Fife and it remained in their ownership until they handed it over to the Ministry of Works in 1928.

Macallan Distillery Visitor Centre

This is the most modern distillery on Speyside, distinguished by the rolling grass 'hillocks' which cover its roof. The visitor tour is also the most 'hi-tech' in the area. Approach it by the A95 heading north and turning left onto the B9102 towards Archiestown.

From Craigellachie the Moray Way follows the track of the old GNoSR Speyside line, with restored stations at Aberlour, Carron, Blacksboat, Ballindalloch, Cromdale and Grantown-on-Spey East. As it leaves Craigellachie, it passes through a former metal-lined railway tunnel under the A941, emerging onto low ground called Collargreen Haugh. The path between Craigellachie and Carron has recently being upgraded as part of a low-carbon transport initiative centred on Aberlour. It proceeds along the east bank of the Spey, giving fine views of Ben Rinnes. On the other side of the road and beyond the woods lies . . .

Walkers' Head Office and Factories

Aberlour is the base of Walkers, the well-known shortbread manufacturers. Largely hidden from view on the path, Walkers' head office at Aberlour House stands high and commands a fine view of the Spey valley and beyond. Aberlour House was once the home of the preparatory school for Gordonstoun which was incorporated into the main Gordonstoun site in 2004. The site of the factories where the shortbread is made is a little further down the road. There is a factory shop but no factory tours.

Haughs and Daughs

As you proceed past Aberlour House, the hilly area to the east is known as the Daugh of Drumferrich. More generally the word 'daugh' denotes a steep area, often as here, a single hillside. In contrast to this a 'haugh' (a word usually, but not exclusively Scottish) is a flat alluvial riverside meadow, commonly found where the river takes a bend. There are several instances of both of these in the Lower Strathspey region, the most famous of which is the Haughs of Cromdale near where the battle was fought in 1690 (see p. 108). The battle's name is something of a misnomer since the region where the rout took place was on somewhat higher ground than that of the river plain.

Aberlour

It may seem surprising to find the prefix 'aber', meaning mouth or estuary, for a place which is far from the sea, but in this context it means 'confluence', that is of the Spey and the Lour Burn, a notable feature of which is the Linn Falls, approached by a detour of about half a mile starting from a signposted path near the distillery to the south of the village. The present village was developed in 1812 by Charles Grant, owner of the neighbouring estate of Elchies who feued 100 plots. Aberlour was at one time well known for its orphanage, founded in 1875 by Margaret Macpherson-Grant and Reverend Charles Jupp,

Aberlour Square.

95

the minister of Craigellachie who was also her personal chaplain. There were further extensions to the orphanage in 1899, and at one time it accommodated over 300 boys and girls, but it was wound up in 1967. However, Aberlour Child Care Trust continued the good work in other ways and is now one of Scotland's main children's charities, providing services throughout Scotland. A prominent building to the east on passing Walkers' factories is St Margaret's Episcopal Church, which was the church used by the orphanage children.

The orphanage was split into two separate units, one for the girls and the other for the boys. Between the two buildings was the school where the children were taught. Only the clocktower of the buildings remains to be seen „just off Mary Avenue. On the north side of the village square stands the parish church with its distinctive tower. This was originally built in 1839, but following a disastrous fire was substantially rebuilt in 1861. The previous pre-Reformation church, dedicated to St Drostan, of which the ruined gable and part of the wall remains, stands in the kirkyard 300 yards to the west.

Aberlour Station

The restored station is currently a visitor information centre and tearoom, staffed seasonally by volunteers from the Aberlour Community Association. An area of open amenity parkland leads down to the Spey. As you leave the station and pass under a railway bridge, glance at the suspension footbridge, a handsome piece of Victorian engineering known as the Penny Bridge, presumably because that was the toll levied on pedestrians. It leads to a pleasant walk back towards Craigellachie on the west side of the river. Prior to the coming of the railway, a ferry service operated over the Spey capable of carrying horses and carts as well as people.

The path from Aberlour to Carron starts by crossing the Burn of Aberlour over another footbridge and continues on a smoothly-surfaced and mostly level track for 3½

*Above, former Aberlour Station. Below, footbridge
over the Lour Burn.*

miles/6km, which makes good cycling and encourages
commuting by road from Carron to Craigellachie.

Turn right when you reach the public road to Carron;
the Speyside Way continues by crossing . . .

Carron Bridge

The railway crossed the Spey at Carron Bridge, built in
1863 to a design by Alexander Gibb, a GNoSR engineer,

97

and fabricated by the iron founders William McKinnon and Co., Aberdeen. Later it carried not only the railway, but the roadway and the footpath which is part of the Moray Way. The main span is a 46-metre arch supported by three cast-iron ribs, each rib cast in seven parts bolted together. The masonry arches on each bank have spans of 7½ metres. It was the last cast-iron railway bridge to be built in Scotland and is a Category A listed building. Just past the bridge is a bicycle repair station, which could prove to be a godsend!

In Carron itself you cannot fail to spot the ultra-modern Dalmunach Distillery, opened in 2015 by Nicola Sturgeon. Opposite, in contrast, are the warehouses of the Imperial Distillery which Dalmunach replaced.

Also opposite Dalmunach lie the Imperial workers' cottages, which when built were models of their kind. The track continues to Knockando following the old railway route. Admire as you go the work of the railway navvies in blasting their way through the rock of Tomdhu, which stands at a particularly swift-flowing part of the Spey. The river seems to dash against the cliff at right angles, which must have made it a particularly hazardous point for the

Carron Bridge.

rafts of the eighteenth-century timber floaters. Next in quick succession come the Knockando and Tamdhu distilleries and Tamdhu platform (see p. 181), from which a worthwhile quarter of a mile detour up the motor road takes you to . . .

Knockando Woolmill

Knockando Woolmill is both a commercial enterprise and a charitable company. Its origins date from the mid-eighteenth century, when a mill was an indispensable part of every rural economy. By 2000 the mill, although still operational and designated a Category A listed building in 1995 along with its machinery, water power system and various outhouses, had fallen into a poor state of repair.

It came to public notice in 1999 as an entry in one of the BBC's *Restoration* programmes, which featured buildings in danger of dereliction but worthy of being preserved. Although it did not win a Restoration award, its appearance set in motion a fundraising campaign led by Dr Jana Hutt, which went from strength to strength. By 2009 the Trust had raised £3.3 million for renovations, and the production of fabric resumed. A grant of £1.3 million from the National Lottery Heritage Fund together with a huge amount of public support had ensured that restoration work could begin. In 2000 the Knockando Woolmill Trust was established and secured ownership of the mill, and in 2017 the Trust was awarded funding by Highlands and Islands Enterprise to allow it to expand its production and workforce.

Support from Scottish Natural Heritage (now Nature-Scot) aimed at setting up a Scottish School of Weaving to keep alive a Scottish artisan tradition, but this ambition was never realised. However skilled volunteers came forward to restore the machinery and buildings to their nineteenth-century state, so the site became part museum and part modern craft works.

The Knockando Woolmill produces a unique tartan, designed in 2010 to commemorate the renovation of the mill. The tartan is registered with the Scottish Register of

Tartans, and may only be manufactured at the Knockando Woolmill.

History of the Mill

The overall site comprises several buildings, all dating to the nineteenth or early twentieth centuries. The mill itself was originally a single-storey rectangular building, and the addition of a two-storey carding and spinning mill led to its current L-plan design. This building contains a number of pieces of historic machinery, including two Victorian looms which are considered to be the oldest such looms still in use.

There are two former dwellings on the site which reflect a high point in the mill's success. The mill house, where the miller's family would have lived, was built around 1910. There is also a cottage, the oldest remaining building on the site dating from the early nineteenth century, a dairy, a winter drying shed, and a purpose-built shop where the mill's produce is sold.

The original owners were Grants, who employed a carder, a spinner and a weaver on the site. At that time farmers would leave a fleece at the mill and return a week or two later to pick it up again as a blanket or garment. In the 1860s, the mill was bought by Alexander Smith, who added some water-powered machinery, although most work was still done by hand. In the 1870s, a 14-foot diameter secondhand water wheel was installed, and in the 1880s a weaving shed was built to house the water-powered loom.

In the early twentieth century, Knockando Woolmill not only served the local market for blankets, tweeds and yarn but also benefited from Ministry of Defence contracts to provide blankets for the armed services during the First World War. Following the war the mill went into decline, although in the late 1940s the waterwheel was disconnected and electric motors were installed to power the machinery.

By the 1960s, most small district mills had either expanded to serve a larger market, or had gone out of

Above, the entrance to the Mill before restoration, and below,
the entrance after restoration.

business. Unusually, Knockando continued to operate
as a local mill, still owned by the company A. Smith and
Son, now under the management of a nephew of the Smith
family called Duncan Stewart. He continued to work at the
mill until 1976, when Hugh Jones, a Welsh entrepreneur
who had come across the site in the course of a motorcycle
tour, bought it, acquired the necessary skills from Duncan
Stewart, and, acting as the sole miller, continued to operate it in the traditional manner for thirty years.

There are two possible derivations for the name Knockando: either it comes from Gaelic *Cnoc Cheannach* meaning

'Hill of Commerce', or, more simply, from *Cnoc dubh* meaning 'Black Hill'. If the latter, then the hill to the west of Tamdhu area, Tom Dow (*Tom* = hillock) effectively has the same name as Knockando. Before leaving Knockando consider a further detour uphill to Upper Knockando, where there are two more noteworthy features in close proximity, Cardhu Distillery (see p. 174) and . . .

Knockando Church

Its circular tower and dominant position make this one of the most picturesquely sited churches in Moray. It was substantially rebuilt in 1906 to replace an inadequate long narrow building, of which one wall remains. Following a fire in 1990, the interior was reconstructed and features a fine modern stained glass window above the pulpit, as well as two windows by the twentieth-century Arts and Crafts designer Douglas Strachan. The church is normally open only for services and events. There are some stones in the graveyard bearing inscriptions in Scandinavian runes. The church of Knockando is united with that of Rothes.

The Speyside Way continues along the west bank of the Spey, with a bridge crossing of the Cally Burn, where you leave the fishing beats of the Knockando estate and continue onwards to . . .

Blacksboat Railway Station

The station building is now a private residence, however there is car parking here which makes this a good entry/exit point for those who choose to walk only a part of the route, particularly as the road bridge, built in 1908, allows it to be accessed from either side of the Spey. Prior to the bridge, Blacksboat was one of the principal foot ferry crossings of the river. A long-serving ferryman operated the service from 1853 to 1900, making an average of around ten crossings a day across the 73m (240 ft) wide river.

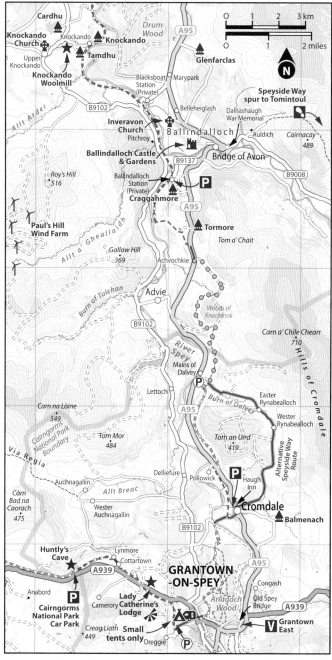

Speyside Way: Knockando to Grantown.

Pitchroy.

As you continue southward, Pitchroy on your right is an impressive shooting-lodge built about 1895, with additions about 1930. (Pronounce the name as *pit-croy* = 'an area of peat' in Pictish Gaelic, one of the relatively few *Pit-* names in Moray.) It was once the home of Captain W. E. Johns, author of the Biggles adventure books. South of Pitchroy there is a further burn crossing by bridge over the *All't a' Gheallaidh* = Burn of the Promise (write your own story line!), and after another mile or so you cross the Spey at . . .

Ballindalloch Railway Bridge

This original railway bridge which now carries the Moray Way is a category-A listed building. It is a wrought-iron lattice girder bridge, with a single span of 59 metres, and plate girder spans at either end giving an overall length of around 75 metres. It was designed by Alexander Gibb who also designed Carron Bridge, with the ironwork fabricated by G. McFarlane of Dundee.

You are now on the east bank of the river and pass a railway-style sign 'Cragganmore', opposite the substantial residential building known as The Granary, built on the site of the old goods yard at Ballindalloch Station whose sidings served Cragganmore Distillery (see p. 177). In spite of the style of the sign there was never a station called Cragganmore, although the west platform of Ball-indalloch Station remains clearly visible as you go past it.

If you are walking or cycling the Moray Way in stages, there is a handy car park next to Ballindalloch Station. This was formerly a hostel operated by Moray Council, but it closed due to problems with the water supply and was then sold in 2012 to a private buyer. However the car park with signage provided by the Council remains, and is a natural entry point to one of the most beauti-ful stretches of the Spey. In 2020 Moray Council were awarded more than half a million pounds by the Low Carbon Transport Fund to upgrade the Speyside Way at this point for all-year-round walking and cycling. The car park is on the right of the B9137 road as you approach from the A95. If you get as far as the distillery you have gone too far!

Ballindalloch Railway Bridge.

Ballindalloch Castle

Ballindalloch Castle is one of the finest surviving examples of a Scottish Baronial castle, and the only stately home open to visitors which is near the Moray Way — but only as the crow flies! The castle has been the home of the Macpherson-Grants from 1546, and the formal grounds were laid out about 1850. Cragganmore is a tantalisingly short distance from the castle, but on the wrong side of the River Avon. Due to the twists and turns in the roads around Ballindalloch, the entrance to the castle is nearly two miles from Ballindalloch Station.

Between Ballindalloch and Cromdale the Speyside Way leaves the river and climbs uphill to a series of forestry paths, first through the Garvault Plantation (from Gaelic *garbh allt* = rough burn), then through the woods of Knockfrink (Gaelic *knoc frangach* = hill of cross-leaved heath), until finally the path opens out to give good views up the valley and a descent towards the riverside at Dalvey.

At around this point you cross a minor public road towards Cromdale (see the alternative route below), and also cross the boundary between the Cairngorm National Park and Moray. This is effectively the boundary between Lower and Upper Strathspey, and in times past this was also a boundary between the largely English-speaking parish of Inveravon and the largely Gaelic-speaking parish of Cromdale. This is also apparent in its placenames. Further possible Gaelic derivations for these are based on advice from a native Gaelic speaker. The village of Cromdale (*Crom dial* = crooked plain) is approached by forestry paths through Tom an Uird, emerging to cross the A95 at Pollowick (*Poll a mhic* = pool of the pig). At this point the two gabbro peaks of the Cromdale Hills come prominently into view; they seem never to have been blessed with English names. The higher one is *Creagan a'Chaise* (= steep rocky place, 722m, 2,367ft) on which the Jubilee Cairn was erected in 1898 (see p. 167). The northerly peak is *Carn a'Ghille Chearr* (= the hill of the left-handed ghillie, 710m, 2,329ft) and is the highest point in Moray. The summit ridge of the Cromdale Hills forms a boundary with the territory of the Glenlivet Crown Estate.

From Pollowick it is a short stroll down the old railway track to . . .

Cromdale Station

This was a small and unprofitable station on the Speyside railway which fell into ruin until in 1994 John Diffey restored it beautifully as a home and workshop, and added a rescued 1916 Great North of Scotland Railway carriage which he reconditioned as holiday accommodation. Just east of the station the track of a railway which served Balmenach Distillery (see p. 175) can still be seen (Balmenach: *Baile meadhonach* = middle farm).

Alternative Route from Dalvey to Cromdale

The minor public road crossed near Dalvey can be followed all the way through to Cromdale via Easter

Cromdale Station.

Shennach, where there is a path leading up to the Cromdale Hills ridge. Compared with the forestry route this gives an option of more open views, at the cost of tramping tarmac underfoot and adding roughly an extra mile to the journey.

Haughs of Cromdale – Site of the Battle (1690)

After the Revolution of 1688 when James VII was dethroned and replaced by William and Mary, the handful of nobles who were in charge of Scottish public affairs were characterised by bigotry, skullduggery, intrigue and corruption. The main division was between the Williamites, mainly nominal Presbyterians, and those loyal to the Stuart dynasty, many of whom, but by no means all, were Catholics. The Grants of Strathspey, in particular the clan chief Sir Ludovick Grant, were strong supporters of the Hanoverian government, although their fellow clansmen, the Grants of Glen Urquhart by Loch Ness, were confirmed Catholics.

The Battles of Killiecrankie, Dunkeld and Cromdale define the so-called Highland Wars in which the Jacobites scored one win, one losing draw and one decisive defeat. However in war, it is the result of the last battle which counts, which is why the Battle of Cromdale was so significant in extinguishing a cause which took 25 years to revive.

The Jacobite defeat came about as their forces, led by Major-General Buchan, were in the process of retreating to the Highlands following the battle of Dunkeld and had chosen to camp in the open ground of the Haughs (i.e. meadows) of Cromdale on 30 April. Word of this reached the Government forces based in Inverness under Sir Thomas Livingston, and although he had orders to await reinforcements from the south, he decided on a swift attack while the Jacobites were at their point of least preparedness. After mustering troops at Brodie Castle near Forres, Livingston's forces marched up over Dava (see Waypoint 16 in section 3, the Dava Way, p. 127) and consolidated at Upper Derraid Farm at about midnight. The men were given the choice to rest or attack. They chose the latter, sweeping past Castle Grant (until 1694 known as Ballachastell) and with the help of Grant scouts crossed the Spey by fords whose whereabouts were known to their spies.

As a battle it probably lasted no more than about 30 minutes – a rout would be a more accurate description – and about 300 to 400 out of 1,500 clansmen were killed. The Jacobites scattered in all directions, and were not effective again as a fighting army until the 1715 rebellion.

Those with an interest in the history of the Jacobite period will want to take a detour of three-quarters of a mile up the minor public road to the site of the battle, which however will not be necessary if they have followed the alternative route above. An interpretation board provides ample information. Lethendy Castle, where some of the Jacobite officers and men were trapped and slaughtered, can be approached by passing through the farmyard. Not much of it remains, and it is not possible to go into it, but with a little imagination it still affords a good view of the route which the Hanoverian forces followed to make their assault. For those prepared to make a longer diversion, a good footpath leads to the Piper's Stone (*Clach nam Piobair*, NJ103269), presumably associated with the battle, which gives another and even better viewpoint all the way down the Spey valley.

Cromdale Church

The church is usually open to visitors for services and also once a week midweek in summer, but at any time you can look for the chiselled mark showing the height of the 1829 floods on the south-east wall. Just past the church the Moray Way crosses the Spey by a road bridge which was created from war surplus material in 1922 and replaced a previous bridge which was washed away in 1921. Upstream you can see some of the piers

The Spey valley from the Piper's Stone.

of a suspension footbridge which was washed away in 1894. The Spey is both wide and relatively shallow at this point, making this one of the main points at which it was forded in the Battle of Cromdale.

Immediately after crossing the river, the Moray Way turns left to enter Anagach Woods beyond which is Grantown. There is a choice of routes here: you can either proceed on the marked paths through the woods, or you can follow the bank of the Spey, passing the pools where Spey oysters were once fished (this is now illegal). In springtime sandwich terns may be seen diving in the river, and stoneflies are active on the bank. After following the river bank you reach a tarmac road which terminates on the left at the old Spey Bridge, constructed

110

by Major Caulfeild (sometimes spelled Caulfield) as part
of Wade's Military Road from Blairgowrie to Fort George.
Follow the tarmac road towards Grantown. Follow a
broad path on the right just beyond the houses to reenter
Anagach Woods and rejoin the marked path.

Alternative Route Bypassing Grantown-on-Spey

The minor public road which crosses the Spey at Cromdale Church turns right following the course of what
once was a road used by the residents of Castle Grant
to get to their church. Follow this road until you come
to a crossroads where the B9102 goes left to Grantown.
Go straight on here, crossing a burn at NJ047299. After
a short distance look for a gate on the right. Go through
this and proceed northwards, with Freuchie Hillock and
then Castle Grant on your left. After 200 yards or so, on
your right there is a monument in a copse to Ian Charles,
the 8th Earl of Seafield. The track which goes round field
edges is boggy but eventually joins a metalled track which
leads past Castle Grant Home Farm to join the Dava Way
at NJ032309.

Anagach Woods

These are woods dominated by a single species, namely
Scots pine, but as the diagram overleaf shows there are
many varieties within the species. In 2002 Anagach Woods
were the subject of a community buy-out from Seafield
estates. Following this the woods have been managed
by the Anagach Woods Trust, led by forestry expert
Basil Dunlop, with the aim of ensuring that they preserve
Strathspey's natural Scots pine heritage.

   The native pinewoods of Anagach, extending for almost 1,000 acres, are exceptional for their wildlife and
fine scenery. The woods have always been much used for
recreation and the Trust has established and maintained
a network of tracks and paths including a stretch of the
Speyside Way. An area at approximately NJ038275 which

was once Grantown's refuse tip is today a clearing, where the various stages in the growth of grassland, heather and regenerating pine seedlings are clearly observable within a compact area.

Anagach (probably from the Gaelic *Can ath gabhach* = 'the dangerous ford') is an area of hillocks and landforms created by a multitude of eskers and moraines laid down when the glaciers melted at the end of the last ice age. These have resulted in the formation of a variety of habitats, from dry heath and pinewood to bogs, which were originally lochs or small lochans, some now populated with bog pine. From suitable vantage points on some of the ridges it is possible to observe in one place many of the different pine varieties.

The original forest disappeared over centuries as the trees were cut for timber or destroyed in forest fires, both wild and deliberate, when even mature trees were burnt. By 1750 this area was no more than a poor rugged piece of heath with sandy soils ill-suited to cultivation, along with extensive peat banks regularly cut by locals for domestic fires. Some evidence of peat-cutting is still visible in the bogs. In 1766 the process of deforestation was reversed when Sir James Grant of Grant, the 'Good

Pine tree varieties (copyright Basil Dunlop).

A path through the Anagach Woods.

Sir James' notable as the founder of Grantown, initiated a plantation of pine, oak and birch with seed gathered from the natural boreal forest remnants of Abernethy and Duthil, and sold to various nurseries and estates throughout Scotland. The seed was also sown in the Castle Grant nursery and so there is little doubt that the origin of the Scots pine that was used for Anagach planting was local.

Through the following century Anagach Woods continued to grow with new plantations, and as the trees matured, early estate records indicate that they were thinned and selectively felled and seedling pines sprang up naturally. Subsequent records and Forestry Society excursion reports testify to how much the estate relied upon natural regeneration to restock the woods after felling, so that the stately pines evident today are almost all regenerated naturally from the original planting. Evidence also confirms that these plantings did indeed originate from the natural pinewoods of Abernethy and Duthil, meaning that their lineage goes all the way back to the trees that colonised Scotland after the last ice age.

If the riverside route from Cromdale is followed, a detour can be made by turning left instead of right at the metalled road and crossing the Spey over the popularly but wrongly called Wade Bridge. This leads in a short distance to Grantown East (see below) and then to the continuation of the Speyside Way (see p. 156) which proceeds for a further 35 miles/56km to its terminus in Newtonmore.

The Old Spey Bridge

This round-arched bridge has three spans of 26, 12 and 6 metres (86, 40 and 20 feet), and it is a tribute to its builders that in the great Moray flood of 1829, only the smallest one was swept away leaving about three feet of the arch which managed to support the parapet. It is said that Peter Grant, a Grantown merchant who customarily traded his goods with the farms on the east bank of the Spey, was determined to continue his usual round, which he did by crawling along the parapet on his hands and knees with his pack on his back. Having landed safely on the other side he was warmly applauded by the onlookers who had gathered!

At the other side of the bridge there is a rather crudely lettered stone, which marks the completion of the bridge by Colonel Charles Hay's regiment.

Grantown East

A Highland Heritage and Cultural Centre opened in 2018 on the site of the former Grantown-on-Spey East Station. It features a pair of carriages of British Rail vintage which have been ingeniously connected together to make a bar and restaurant. The centre itself is in the rebuilt station and has static displays as well an amply-stocked shop.

From here you may either retrace your steps to return to Grantown via Anagach Woods, or proceed along the A95 using the elegant A95 bridge built in 1931 which leads to Grantown after half a mile.

Once in Grantown the Moray Way continues westward from the Anagach Woods car park, and crosses the High Street near the Cooperative store where it becomes part of

Grantown-on-Spey East Station.

the Dava Way. Several detours are possible in Grantown, one of several planned towns which came into being towards the end of the eighteenth century as a consequence of the Scottish Enlightenment.

Grantown-on-Spey

Grantown, as the name implies, is the home territory of Clan Grant. It owes its existence to clan chief Sir James Grant who laid it out as a planned town to the south of his castle on a virgin site in 1765 and 1766. Sir James conceived it as an industrial centre that would help to overcome destitution in the surrounding area with mills and factories, schools, a hospital and so on. (Grantown's hospital, named after Ian Charles Grant, the 8th Earl of Seafield, was closed in 2021 as facilities have now been concentrated in a new hospital in Aviemore.) By 1797 Grantown was a post town (a town with a main post office) with around 300 inhabitants. From 1814 a coach between Perth and Inverness called at Grantown, and in 1819 the Grant Arms in the Square was opened as a coaching inn en route to Elgin, a development which helped the town to grow and prosper. Like Forres and Lossiemouth, it

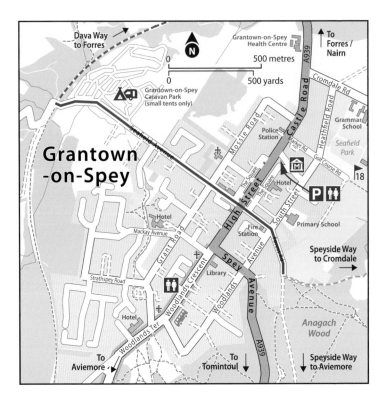

boasts a Mercat Cross, only this one didn't appear until 2015, when its reconstruction outside the Town House was part of Grantown's 250th year celebrations. The present 4-star Grant Arms is one of the Highlands' most popular centres for wildlife tours. Many of the buildings in the centre of the town were built in the Victorian or early twentieth-century era when the coming of the railways helped boost Grantown's reputation as one of Scotland's most fashionable holiday destinations. The former Palace Hotel on the south-east corner of the square, now a care home, typified the splendour of that age.

The ski-ing boom in the Cairngorms in the 1950s and 60s helped to revive the tourist economy, and more recently has made it popular with a wide range of holidaymakers. Inverallan Church, built in 1884 in memory of Ian Charles, the 8th Earl of Seafield and chief of Clan Grant, is a light and airy building approached by a pleasant tree-lined avenue from the Square. The headquarters of the Cairngorm National Park Association (CNPA) is also here on this road.

In September 1860 Queen Victoria and Prince Albert visited Grantown in one of their longer expeditions by coach from Balmoral. They travelled incognito and stopped overnight. The Queen described the place as 'a long straggling toun'. They spent the night in what they called 'Hotel Grantown' which was almost certainly the Grant Arms as it was then. Although they brought their

Above, the Grant Arms where Queen Victoria slept in 1860, and below, where she would have slept today...

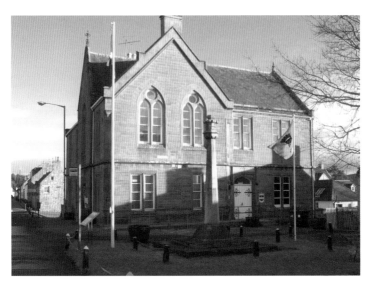

Grantown Town House and Mercat Cross.

own wine, the dinner was 'very fair, all very clean — soup, hodge-podge, mutton broth with vegetables, fowl with white sauce, good roast lamb, very good potatoes, besides one or two other dishes which I did not taste, ending with a good tart of cranberries.'

The following day they visited Lord Seafield in Castle Grant – 'a plain-looking house like a factory'. When they drove back through Grantown word had got out and everyone was in the street, the landlady at the Grant Arms waved her handkerchief and the ringletted maid waved a flag from the window. In spite of that the coachman 'did not observe or guess anything' as to the identity of his passengers!

Castle Grant, the ancestral home of the chiefs of Clan Grant, lies to the north of the town. Its original name was Castle Freuchie, and a hamlet, Castletown of Freuchie, lay under its shadow. The name Freuchie dates from the fifteenth century when the Barony of that name was bestowed on Sir Duncan Grant by the Earl of Moray. The castle was also known as Ballachastell (from Gaelic = *the castle of the township*) which is how it was shown on maps depicting the Battle of Cromdale in 1690. In 1694 the name of Freuchie was dropped in favour of Castle Grant, and the castle itself was extensively rebuilt as a mansion house in 1765. It is approached by a long drive with a turreted lodge visible from the A95. It is also visible from the Moray Way as Lady Catherine's Halt (see p. 122) is approached. Castle Grant has had a chequered recent history, including being opened briefly as the centre of a theme park, then owned for a short time by Craig Whyte, whose chequered business career included at one time ownership of Rangers football club, and then by a Russian oligarch. It remains privately owned and is not open to the public.

Full details of Grantown's past and present can be found in . . .

The Grantown Museum

This independent and engaging museum features the highest standards of contemporary museum design and display in describing the history of Grantown and its inhabitants. In particular there is much detail about Sir James Grant's original plans of 1765 for creating a planned village in the spirit of the Enlightment, and how these are still reflected in the appearance of the present-day town. There are also items and artefacts relating to the history of Clan Grant and its chiefs who built and inhabited Castle Grant, and who in some cases were prominent figures in the national affairs of Scotland. The museum also has a good stock of local books and other items for sale. There is a charge for admission.

From the Co-operative store at the corner of Grantown Square follow the brown sign down Seafield Road past the caravan park to the start of the Dava Way at Dulicht Bridge.

3
THE DAVA WAY

The Dava Way, north from Grantown, marks a complete change in character from both the Moray Coast Trail and the Speyside Way. It was described by Radio Scotland as Scotland's most family-friendly long-distance trail – not too surprising, since once the traveller from Grantown-on-Spey to Forres has made the four-mile ascent to Dava Moor, the return to Forres is downhill more or less all the way! The track is well signposted and waymarked, and as it largely follows the remains of old railway track, little detailed direction as to the route is necessary. There is a sequence of eighteen information boards at selected waypoints along the route which spell out different aspects of its story. A summary of these follows (they are numbered from Forres going south) which give a better picture of the route than simple step-by-step directions.

The name Dava may be a variant of *davach* – a Pictish Gaelic land measure based on productive capacity rather than dimensions, which was once used as a basis for taxation. It seems to have meant the amount of land which was sufficient to grow enough for a tub of grain at harvest, thus the size varied according to the quality of the soil, but on average being about 400 acres.

On joining the Dava Way near Dulicht Bridge on the outskirts of Grantown, the track passes a flat area called the Mossie, which was where Joseph Mitchell, the civil engineer who oversaw the construction of many Highland railways, wished to site Grantown's railway station. This would have had the further advantage of being a junction point with the track of the Great North of Scotland Railway which was simultaneously being constructed on its way down the Spey. However the then Seafield Estates' factor, Colonel Dixon , who lived close to the Mossie, disliked

Opposite: Along the Dava Way.

121

A cutting north of Grantown.

railways, which he saw as a menace to frighten the grouse! The result was that Grantown finished up with two stations a mile apart, and the two railways didn't meet until they reached Boat of Garten.

Beyond the Mossie the railway went through a deep cutting before emerging onto an embankment with a farm called Lynmacgregor to the west (*lyn* = Gaelic 'enclosure') which suggests that there may have been MacGregors hereabouts, in spite of their being traditionally viewed by those in Grant lands as cattle thieves. Just before Waypoint 18 the Dava Way is crossed by a road servicing the proposed Ourack windfarm (see p. 204).

WAYPOINT 18 (NJ032302)
Lady Catherine's Halt

The architecturally fine bridge over the A939 was designed to complement the East Lodge of Castle Grant. Its style is the same as that of Scurrypool Bridge at Waypoint 2 (see p. 153). The lodge building and its passenger halt were built by the Inverness and Perth Junction Railway as a condition for securing permission from the Earl of Seafield to cross his territory.

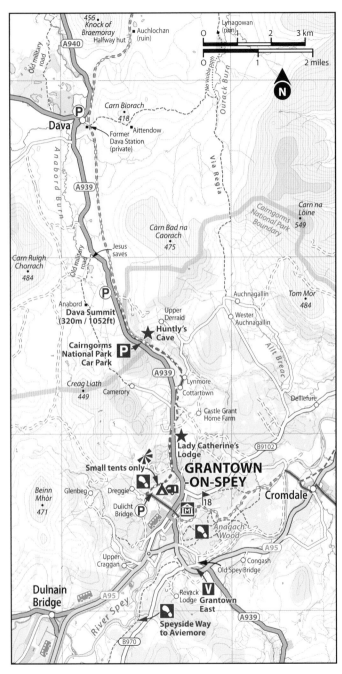

Dava Way: Grantown to Dava Viaduct.

Lady Catherine's Lodge.

The name 'Lady Catherine' is a mystery, perhaps an invention, since it is not a name which features in the Grant dynasty. The Lodge had a platform for the convenience of the Laird of Grant when using the trains. When the Dowager Countess of Seafield died at Cullen in 1911, her coffin was brought here by rail to lie in state in Castle Grant, before being moved to its last resting place in the family vault at Duthil. The spiral staircase in the Lodge proved impossible to negotiate, and so the coffin was slid secretively and unceremoniously down the embankment, prior to loading onto the waiting hearse.

The Dava Way leaves the old railway track shortly after Waypoint 18, and continues alongside fields and then through mixed woodland close to the A939 until a junction with a minor public road leading to the Braes of Castle Grant is reached. The Dava Way follows this road

124

for a quarter of a mile, giving good views of the Cromdale Hills (see p. 166), to a signpost directing walkers into another predominantly coniferous wood. After a further half mile, you rejoin the railway track, with the view now eastward to Upper Derraid Farm and the valley which Hanoverian men and horses traversed on their way to the Battle of Cromdale (see Waypoint 16, p. 127).

WAYPOINT 17 (NJ024326)
Huntly's Cave

The Huntly family were committed followers of Charles I in the mid-seventeenth century. After a defeat of the Royalists by the Marquis of Argyll, the second Marquis is said to have concealed himself for some days in a cleft in the flat rocks at the top of the cliff. Later his son Lewis Gordon, third Marquis of Huntly, also hid here after deserting the Marquis of Montrose in 1644, a defection which has never been satisfactorily explained. What is more certain is that Mary Grant, sister of the Laird of Grant, sustained him by sending supplies from Castle Grant, thereby leading to their marriage and the subsequent birth of the first Duke of Gordon.

The entrance to Huntly's Cave.

The main exposed vertical cliff consists of schistose blocks characteristic of the foliated metamorphic rocks — rocks with distinctive patterning and layers — which dominate this area. These represent sediments from an ancient seabed which were transformed during what is known as the Caledonian mountain-building episode between 450 and 495 million years ago. Scotland and England smashed into each other as the Lapetus Ocean closed. The consequent heat and pressure caused the foliation, flattening and drawing out the constituent minerals in parallel layers. Nearby are granitic rocks which represent the remnants of volcanoes also associated with the upheavals of that time, as the tectonic plate on which England was carried melted on its descent beneath Scotland.

As the track emerges from the woods into the open moor, the foundations of railway workers' cottages can still be discovered by careful search.

 Stories handed down say that as the trains headed along the line, judicious shovelfuls of coal helped keep the fireplaces of the railway workers fuelled, in return for which bottles of beer in wire containers were loaded into the engine drivers' cabs. The railway was also used to

On the descent over Huntly's Cave.

Dava Way Association volunteers at work on the moor.

take the Dava children to and from school in Grantown, and the newspapers were delivered on the return journey. Aristocratic guests at Tulchan Lodge on Speyside continued to hunt on the moor as their ancestors had done ever since the fourteenth century. On one occasion a railwayman and his wife were sitting down to their tea when a knock was heard on the door, whereupon the visitor announced 'I'm the king!' (Edward VII). A sugar bowl and milk jug were presented to the couple by a courtier to commemorate the occasion.

WAYPOINT 16 (NJ016339)
Dragoons Route to Cromdale

The Land Rover track to the east used for estate purposes climbs steadily following a route which once brought Dava Moor into the spotlight of Scotland's national history. At dead of night on 1 May 1690, a party of Government foot-soldiers (musketeers) and cavalry (dragoons) led by Sir Thomas Livingston made their way over Dava Moor with the aim of putting paid to the Jacobite forces which had encamped above Cromdale the previous evening (see more about the Haughs of Cromdale on p. 108).

The view from Waypoint 15 towards Dava.

To the south lies the rounded hill *Carn-na-Croiche* or Hanging Hill. In the seventeenth and eighteenth centuries cattle reiving (stealing) was an established practice and the ravine by Huntly's Cave was an excellent spot at which to ambush reivers from Lochaber and Badenoch returning with their booty. In 1670, one of the Grants pursued the reivers to their hideout, but was spotted and shot dead with a musket. The killer was brought to justice and condemned to death on the Hanging Hill gallows where other reivers had met a similar fate. One managed to swallow some poison on the route to the gallows, but his dead body was hanged just the same and buried nearby. For many years afterwards people came to drink from the suicide's skull. This was believed to be effective in curing epilepsy, and the skull itself was always carefully restored to the grave.

Shortly beyond Waypoint 16 lies the restored summit sign at 1052 feet/320 metres above sea level. Although the path seems to continue to a higher summit at Waypoint 14, this is an illusion, and the true summit is correctly marked. The path leads straight to Waypoint 14, passing . . .

WAYPOINT 15 (NJ013350)
The Dava Skeleton

In 1927 a labourer digging for peat on Dava Moor, six miles or so north of Grantown, came across a buried skeleton judged to be about 200 years old. Some pieces of clothing attached to the skull led to speculation that it was the body of a Highland soldier returning from Culloden. News spread and the story began to circulate that what had been discovered was the ceremonial burial of a Highland chieftain. Eventually the bones were sent to Edinburgh for expert analysis. Several weeks later the report came back saying that the body was that of a weak 20-year-old female not more than four feet ten inches in height. Diggers now are more intent on keeping the track as dry as possible for walkers and cyclists!

WAYPOINT 14 (NJ011365)
Heatherbell Cutting

There were three major incidents hereabouts when the railway was blocked with snow. The first was in 1865 and lasted for a week, which stimulated the Inverness and Perth Junction Company to design the first railway snowploughs. The next major blockage was for nine days in 1883 when most of a trainload of 33 bullocks and 54 pigs perished. The third blockage occurred in the severe

Ten-day line blockage in the winter of 1962-3.

Train arriving at Dava Station.

winter of 1962-63. On 6 February 1963 a southbound train left Forres at noon but became derailed in a heavy drift thirteen feet high. A large snowplough built around a tender and powered by two engines made a charge at the drift but was overturned, and both locomotives were derailed. The twenty passengers on the train were eventually rescued and taken back to Forres shortly before midnight.

Looking southwards there are good views of the northern summits of the Cairngorms as the path continues over near level ground to . . .

WAYPOINT 13 (NJ008387)
Dava South

In early days the high moor belonged to the Comyns (later the name became Cummings) whose stronghold was the island castle of Lochindorb, two miles or so to the west. Lochindorb was home to the notorious Wolf of Badenoch, younger brother of the Scottish King Robert III. After being excommunicated for either adultery, land seizure or both, he wreaked personal revenge on the Bishop of Moray in 1390 by marching with a force from Lochindorb to set fire to Elgin Cathedral, with a bit of additional casual arson in Forres along the way!

In the thirteenth and fourteenth centuries, the English Kings Edward I and Edward III marched into the north of Scotland with mighty invading armies. They also found this to be a splendid hunting area, abounding in red and roe deer, wolves, foxes, wildcats, pine martens and pole-cats, as well as many kinds of wildfowl.

Dava was one of the remotest working stations in the LMS network. It had a passing loop and in the picture shown opposite the porter and the driver have just ex-changed the purses containing tokens which granted authorisation to proceed on single stretches of line. Only one driver at a time could hold a token for each such stretch of line, so there was no danger of two trains ap-proaching from opposite directions.

There are so many stores of furtive redistributions of Highland Railway coal that one wonders how any ever got through to run the engines. Once a newly-joined young apprentice at Forres was sent to Dava to look af-ter the station as a locum for the stationmaster who was about to go on leave. On his first night he was terrified by a loud rumbling sound, and on looking out observed a large man shovelling coal to take away from the yard on

Dava Station in its heyday.

Dava Inn.

a wheelbarrow. Although too timid to challenge him at the time, he accosted him next day and asked him, 'Will you be back the night for mair, Davie?' That evening after dark Davie, suitably shamed, came back to return the coal!

Dava Schoolhouse

The old schoolhouse reopened its doors to the public for bed and breakfast in 2016, and is reached by a minor detour. Inside the owners have recreated something of the character of the old schoolroom in the dining room. Years before that, Dava Inn, which lay a short distance away, was a staging post for mail from the south, as the artist's impression above shows.

The Battle of Dava Moor

The small population of Dava in the late nineteenth century was a mixture of indigenous farming folk and railwaymen on the one hand and travellers on the other. Just across the road from the schoolhouse there was a busy coaching inn which in 1871 was the scene of a bloody confrontation. Amongst the regular but least profitable customers was a band of itinerant workers. One night their refusal to pay their bill caused the burly, hospitable innkeeper to reach for his gun. Although he was rapidly disarmed, word got around and a party of local lads was organised to come to his rescue with clubs and shinty sticks. They were royally entertained for their trouble and unanimously declared their willingness to undertake the

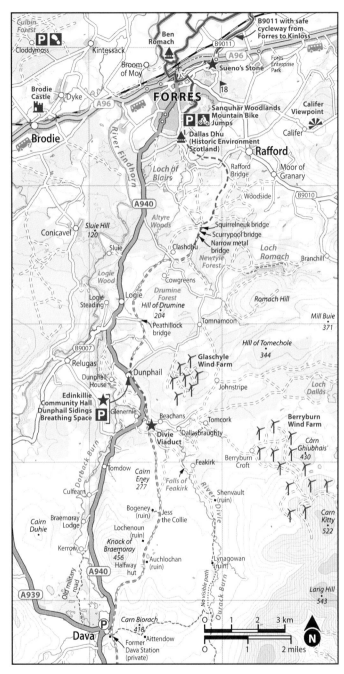

Dava Way north: Dava to Forres.

Diversion at the Dava Station sign.

same duty, provided the reward in the aftermath was on a similar scale!

At this point there is a diversion leading away from the old railway station at a point where the restored Dava Station sign has been erected.

Continue for a short distance along a broad gravel road to a T-junction, at which take the left turn. The right turn leads to a group of privately owned houses, one of which is the old station building. Proceeding down the left track look for a signpost which directs walkers (but not cyclists!) through some conifer woods, mainly spruce. Cyclists and horses must continue onto the A940 until a signpost directs them to join up with walkers on the railway track at a point just south of a metal gate just before Waypoint 12.

At this point you cross several boundaries, first that between Highland and Grampian regions, also those of the counties of Inverness-shire and Moray, the parishes of Cromdale and Edinkillie, and the Seafield and Moray Estates. Within Moray you are now in the local government area of Finderne (see p. 7, not to be confused with Findhorn), one of the most thinly populated areas in

Moray within which the whole of the remainder of the
Dava Way lies, and through which the Dava Way is its
major off-road highway.

WAYPOINT 12 (NJ008391)
Transport and Roads

Following the 1745 rebellion General Wade built a military
road from Blairgowrie to Fort George which went through
Dava. From Dava to Forres there was a non-military road
which was improved successively by the Turnpike Acts
of 1766, Thomas Telford's master plan of 1801 for roads
in the Highlands, and the numerous reports of the Highlands Roads and Bridges Commission, set up in 1803.
Carriages in the form of small horsedrawn carts were in
common use by the reasonably wealthy inhabitants, who
paid tolls at tollhouses such as at Dava. The mail service
was very important — Grantown and Forres had post
offices in 1781, with a runner employed to carry the mails
between them, the first regular walker on the Dava Way!
Goods too were conveyed by carriers using ponies who
braved all weathers.

The later railway building has given rise to its share
of ghost stories, given that the moor is an area where

Ponies carrying goods northwards in the snow.

The ghost train!

darkness is intense. One cold snowy winter's night in 1917, John Macdonald was returning from Dunphail to Dava when a shimmering locomotive and four trucks rushed past him, with smoke pouring from its chimney. The best explanation offered for the apparition was that thirty years earlier a train of cattle wagons had caught fire at Dava Station and all the animals perished. In 1949 one Mrs Macdonald, who lived in one of the moorland crofts, walked along the same line to visit her sister who was ill in Dunphail. As she approached home on her return journey she thought she could hear a train coming up the line even though she knew there were no more due that night. Nevertheless she looked over her shoulder and was confronted by a grey train in full steam. It raced through the night and although the footplate was deserted the fierce glow of the firebox was reflected in the pall of steam and smoke from the chimney, with the brightly-lit carriages streaming behind two feet off the ground. These and similar events are commemorated in a biennial Ghost Train walk from Grantown to Forres, which takes place overnight on a weekend in midsummer. A restaurant tent at Edinkillie provides a welcome distraction from the supernatural tensions of the night as daylight begins to dawn.

The path proceeds east round the Knock of Braemoray (1492 ft/455m) which is prominent ahead, parting company with the A940 which goes round it to the west. There is no clear path to the summit from the Dava Way, and the initial stages are boggy. If you wish to make a detour by climbing the Knock it is best to do so from a layby on the A940 opposite Kerrow Farm. The boggy area is vividly colourful in summer, with white bog cotton, yellow bog asphodel, light blue harebells, purple cross-leaved heath and stands of heath spotted orchids.

The Knock of Braemoray was once conquered by Mrs Margaret Thatcher in the course of one of her private visits to Lord Laing of Dunphail when he was Treasurer of the Conservative party. The then Prime Minister declined all offers of boots or other outdoor clothing and insisted on going up the hill just as she was in the clothes and shoes she was wearing (which she did!).

As you continue round a broad curve, the next feature reached is . . .

WAYPOINT 11 (NJ021413)
The Halfway Hut

This is a former railwaymen's hut which the Dava Way Association took pride in making into a mini-bothy, with

The Halfway Hut.

137

Anne Matheson, the last resident of Auchenlochan.

triggered lighting from solar panels. It lies at a point roughly halfway between Dava and Dunphail and also roughly halfway between Grantown and Forres. Entries in the visitors' book show that pre-Covid, about 50% of visitors were relatively local, about 25% came from further afield in Scotland, and the remaining 25% came from Europe or overseas.

An outline of stones a short distance to the north on the opposite side of the track marks what used to be the farm of Auchenlochan. Its last recorded occupation was in the 1901 census. Large families were common then; for example Anne Matheson, a shepherd's wife, brought up a family of nine young children here from the 1880s onward. Her grandson was well-known in Moray as an entertainer under the name of 'The Singing Molecatcher'. People who lived on the moor had to be hardy. Children from some outlying farms walked up to fourteen miles a day to attend the schools at Dunphail and Dava. The majority of the farm families and servants on the moor were born in Edinkillie parish, or, if not, in one of the adjacent parishes. By contrast the itinerant folk (tinkers, so called because they sold pots and pans) who lived up at Dava came from parishes all over Scotland.

A series of three ponds lie beyond the ruins, where greylag geese often bring up their young, and wigeon may breed. At times of migration any large V-shaped skeins seen overhead are likely to be pink-footed geese. In a good year, short-eared owls may be observed on the high moor.

As you proceed northward the ruins of Lochenoun are just visible north of the track before it continues into a wide cutting, at the end of which, to the east, lies . . .

WAYPOINT 10 (NJ025428)
Bog Causeway

The railway builders crossed a small lochan here by means of a causeway. To the east lies a marshy area which in spring comes to life with bogbean and marsh cinquefoil. The water is over a metre deep in the middle of the bog where the thick stems of water horsetail dominate. What appears to be solid ground is in fact a 'quaking bog' – try it with caution!

The 'quaking bog'.

This small area in which ground transitions from pond to solid land demonstrates an evolutionary succession of plant life, beginning with the bogbeans and rushes, then sedges, next heather, and finally pine and willow seedlings (compare this with another botanical progression in Anagach Woods, see p. 111).

This miniature landscape provides a glimpse into a larger area of 930 acres lying to the south and east of the railway track, known as Moidach More. This is one of about 240 blanket bogs in Scotland which are protected as Special Areas of Conservation (SACs). Blanket bogs such as Moidach More support a significant amount of peat-forming vegetation such as *Sphagnum*, *Eriophorum* (cotton-grasses) and *Calluna vulgaris* (heather). Blanket bogs are formed in a climate of high rainfall combined with low rates of evaporation through plant leaves. Peat develops over large expanses of undulating ground which are thus blanketed to varying depths.

WAYPOINT 9 (NJ026432)
Bogeney

The ruins to the west are the deserted farm buildings of Bogeney, the most recently occupied of the ruins on the moorland section of the line. The original inhabitants, who scratched fields out of the moor, lived in single-storeyed turf huts in which the farmer, his wife, servants and any children lived and fed together around a single fire at one end with beasts occupying the other. An interior of this sort is reconstructed in the Findhorn museum at Logie Steading, which is a popular retail and restaurant centre lying approximately a mile off route, reached by a detour along the A940 from the Edinkillie Breathing Place.

Jess the Collie

In the last century Bogeney Farm was occupied by a Mrs Macdonald, a widow whose husband worked all his life on the railway. When he died she continued to work the farm on her own, always welcoming visitors and offering

Ruins of farm buildings at Bogeney.

strangers hospitality. She got her shopping by giving notes to the postman who passed them on to the shopkeepers in Grantown who in turn made up parcels with a special kind of knot and delivered them to Grantown West Station. The train driver on the early northbound train then collected the Bogeney newspapers at Aviemore and Mrs Macdonald's parcels at Grantown. When he approached Bogeney he slowed down and blew his whistle, whereupon her faithful collie Jess ran down to receive the delivery – possibly the earliest recorded example of literally 'online shopping'.

From Waypoint 12 onwards you have been passing through the parish of Edinkillie, but it is only now that some of its dwellings start to appear in the distance. It will be obvious that from an agricultural point of view the land around you before you enter Bantrach Wood is of a relatively poor upland kind.

WAYPOINT 8 (NJ026438)
Bogeney North Bridge

This is the first point from which wind turbines can be seen: Berry Burn wind farm to the east (29 turbines) and Glaschyle to the north (12 turbines).

Dava Moor in autumn – note the wind turbines.

There is a permanent hill flock of about 800 grazing sheep on the moor, and an important part of looking after them is the control of ticks. These can spread Lyme's Disease which can affect sheep and wildlife as well as walkers. Typically, sheep here are washed for ticks every eight weeks during the summer grazing period between April and October. After this time they are moved to winter grazing down the hill, where weather conditions are generally more clement. On this lower ground, both grass and forage crops are grown to support the sheep through the winter.

The bridge which crosses the Burn of Newton not only carried the railway but also passed over a grassy platform which provided a means of moving livestock from one part of the moor to another without them having to cross the railway line. The source of the Burn lies in a ravine which was said to be the site of the lair of the last wolves in Edinkillie. They were killed in an audacious raid on their den on Cairn Eney in the early eighteenth century. Two brothers from Feakirk Farm set about the task. While one of them hunted for the wolves, the other was set to watch the den, but panicked and fled when the wolf returned with her cubs. He covered himself in blood and told everyone that his brother had been killed, but the lie was exposed when his brother returned later. The result was that he was summarily tried by the local baron bailie and hanged for cowardice.

WAYPOINT 7 (NJ024456)
South End of Bantrach Wood and Timber Felling

The woodland here is managed by Dunphail estate to the east and Glenernie estate to the west. The current planting dates from around 1960 and consists largely of pine, with some Japanese larch on the perimeter. As with many forestry plantations in Scotland the Bantrach Wood was completely clearfelled to help meet the nation's timber needs during the Second World War. After the War it became open ground for grazing and supported about 160 head of sheep. Recently there has been timber-felling on both sides of the old railway, which will aid the growth of quality timber. If you are looking south, heather moorland lies to the east and farmland to the west. This area is managed by Dunphail estate, primarily as a grouse moor of around

A grouse butt on Dava Moor in earlier times.

143

A ganger's tablet.

12,000 acres. Although there have not been any grouse shoots for several decades, habitat management remains important. Predator control forms an important part of the estate's work, which benefits not only grouse but also mountain hares, curlew, lapwings, golden plover and other wildlife which can be seen at different seasons.

The patchwork-quilt effect on the moor arises from systematic heather burning between September and April. The older heather provides nesting cover and shelter from weather and predators, while the regenerating shoots of the burnt area act as a food supply during the nesting period. Individual grouse territories will often contain both new and old heather areas.

As the viaduct is approached, about forty yards south of it, careful search in the grass on the west side of the track will reveal a small concrete tablet (see illustration), dating from the LMS railway days, which the gangers used to check that the rails had not shifted in the ballast on a curve where trains could potentially stress the rails. In the example shown the 30 would be the distance in inches from the notch to the nearest rail, and the 2½ inches is the cant between each rail. A second tablet lies about 20 yards further north. The distance between rails would have been rigidly checked with very small tolerances, and the ganger would also have carried a 4ft 8½in standard gauge to check the track width.

With such precautions rail passengers in the LMS days must never have had any fears about crossing the viaduct; however, in the early days of the Highland Railway things were a little different. A story is told of a Forres contractor who took his gang of workmen each morning to a job at Dava. One day, to save his having to make the journey to collect them at day's end, he told them to take the train home. As it rattled at speed over the viaduct, one of the older workers looked with trepidation over the parapet and exclaimed 'What a terrible way to go to eternity wi' a week's wages unpaid!'

WAYPOINT 6 (NJ022461)
South End of Divie Viaduct

The Divie Viaduct, which cost around £10,000 to build in 1861, was bought by the late Lord Laing of Dunphail for £90 to prevent its demolition when the railway closed. Its recent partial repointing cost over £100,000, and even

The Divie Viaduct.

The former Edenkillie manse.

now (in 2022) it requires a further £200,000 of repairs! The seven-arch viaduct towers 106 feet/32m above the Divie valley and is a total of 477 feet/144m in length.

To the west, in the valley below the viaduct, lies Edinkillie Church. Its former manse was built in 1823 to a striking 'swept wing' plan designed by the architect John Robertson of Elgin in the style of William Playfair. Edinkillie Church itself was built in 1741 and improved in 1813. It is bright and pleasing in the traditional eighteenth-century style with a central pulpit and galleries on three sides. Edinkillie Church is linked with the church of Dyke to the west of Forres, with further linkages inevitable under current parish reorganisation within the Church of Scotland.

As you look to the south specimens of virtually all the common conifer and native broadleaf species to be found in the Highlands can be seen. The conifers are predominantly Sitka spruce and Norway spruce. To the south of the Divie, a line of Japanese larch are taller than the spruces immediately behind them. Beyond this is a plantation of Scots pine, and in the valley itself and along the trackside to the north there are silver birch, various willows, alder, hazel, oak, ash, sycamore, rowan and gean (wild cherry). The viaduct marks a transition point between the rugged moorland which dominates the Dunphail estate and the gentler mix of farmland and woodland which characterises Logie estate towards the north.

As you go through what are now the less rugged parts of Edinkillie parish, the Dava Way as far as Waypoint 5 runs along the border between Dunphail and Logie estates before heading through the latter. You may want to pause and contrast the relative lack of human presence today with the activity and bustle which were part of life here around the 1790s, when the minister of the parish made the following insightful contribution to the *Statistical Account of Scotland*, published in 1793:

The farms are very small (rentals £3–£10 p.a. – compare with Castle Grant rental of £2,000 p.a.) which accounts for the low state of farming in the parish. There is little industry among the men except for preparing and carrying peats to Forres. The women are diligent spinners, an employment introduced by the late Dr Patrick Cumming of the nearby estate of Relugas who negotiated with SSPCK (Scottish Society for the Promotion of Christian Knowledge) for the establishment of a school with a salaried schoolmistress.

People travel to Forres regularly and buy the greatest part of their necessities at the markets there. They also have the opportunity to sell their own handmade goods there of which there are very few. There are enough weavers and tailors in Edinkillie to make it self-sufficient in clothing. Also there are 2 shoemakers, 4 coopers, 10 riddlemakers, and almost every man in the parish is a cartwright. Carts are made of alder and birch and supply Elgin and Forres markets at prices ranging from 6/- to 21/- . There are four distilleries which sell spirits as fast as they can be produced, most of it going to Strathspey and Badenoch. The revenue officers have been successful in bringing a total stop to smuggling on the northern coasts which used to be a source of supply of foreign spirits.

Edinkillie's inhabitants are in general sober, peaceable and honest in dealings, although more liquor is consumed by younger people than is good for their health or morals. The poor fund is very small, not exceeding £5 per annum accrued from church collections and donations from wealthy residents. Edinkillie's inhabitants are of a charitable disposition and are always willing to assist those in distress. All of the inhabitants are of the established religion with no sectaries, although in general their attitude to religion is gloomy. Scotch dialect was heard in the lower parts of the parish, Gaelic in the upper. 50 years previously the minister preached half the time in English and the other half in Gaelic.

The population increased from 1,443 in 1755 to 1,800 in 1793. It still seems to be on the increase since a good deal of the waste land in the remoter parts of the parish has lately been brought into culture by families settling in the wilder parts of it. Many people live to a great age, a few over 90.

Agriculture: There are a considerable number of black cattle in the parish, larger than Highland cattle, and many are used in the plough. Horses are small and of indifferent quality. Most tenants keep a few sheep, but management of them is not well understood. Only the ancient white-faced breed is to be found which provide fine wool and excellent mutton. There are many foxes.

The great proportion of the parish is moor and moss. The only kinds of grain are barley, Scotch bear [bere], oats and rye. Every tenant plants a few potatoes for his own use. Black or grey oats are much preferred to white because they produce more straw for fodder. Farming in general is in a very wretched state. Grain crops are often repeated in the same fields four or five times in succession until the land hardly returns the feed, then has to lie fallow. Proper rotation has been demonstrated by some gentlemen, but hitherto has not had any effect to improve the practice of common farmers. Adding lime would be very desirable, but although this is available in local quarries, cost is a deterrent. Problems of this sort may be due to short leases typically of 19 years which deters tenant farmers from making substantial improvements to their holdings. By contrast agriculture in the adjoining parish of Cromdale is considerably more enlightened with the major landowners embracing the new ideas such as crop rotation and the application of lime.

A famine in 1782 followed by considerable early snowfalls led to severe hardship and a period of inflation which made things worse. The social hierarchy on the land at this time consisted of tacksmen, who came next below and held leases from the great landowners, such as the Earl of Moray. Next in rank came the smaller farmers who also held tenancies on lease, then below these came servants who suffered most as the farmers sought to reduce their numbers in a time of soaring wages. The class of day-labourers got little if any employment.

Around this time work started on breaking in waste land in the remoter parts of the parish. This was driven by families displaced from land in the more fertile parts of Moray, as landowners and tacksmen began to pioneer the new and less labour-intensive agricultural techniques which came about in the period of the Scottish Enlightenment.

Poor Relief in the Nineteenth Century

The Poor Law Boards met every half year to update the roll of paupers and their allowances. Forres at the time had a 'School of Female Industry' and employed a salaried Inspector of the Poor. Poor relief was supported by church collections, and as well as this wealthy residents contributed regularly, sometimes by cash donations, at other times by donations of money, clothes, tea and coal. In the middle years of the nineteenth century the coming of the railways led to the abolition of duty on sea-borne coal, so that loads from Newcastle were shipped to

Inverness and transported onward by rail. This made heating houses both more affordable for people in the Highlands generally and was much less labour-intensive than peat.

In the nineteenth century tea was seen as a considerable luxury. In 1885 a concert was held in order to provide a pound of tea for each poor person; in 1897 Mr and Mrs Lindsay, Edinkillie emigrants, despatched a gift of tea from India for distribution in the parish. Tea was not always seen as an unalloyed blessing – in the neighbouring parish of Dyke and Moy its use was reported as 'making alarming progress among many who need better nourishment at less expense'.

On the west side of the path, just beyond where two tracks cross, lies the former Dunphail school and schoolhouse, to which children from some of the remote crofts on the moor used to trek several miles each way every day. For a while it operated as the Braemoray Inn. The path continues through an area of largely semi-mature woodland, bypassing the privately owned Dunphail Station, the platform and restored station sign of which are clearly visible on the west side of the track. Between here and Waypoint 5 you will have experienced a sharp contrast between the harshness of the moor and the gentle fertility of the Moray plain.

WAYPOINT 5 (NJ015483)
Laurels Bridge

This is so-called because 'The Laurels' is the name of the house whose garden adjoins the path. The Breathing Place immediately to the south was established in 2008 following a BBC initiative giving grants to redevelop neglected industrial sites as green scenic areas to benefit both people and nature. There are picnic tables and a simple path network, with information boards covering aspects of the planting work and wildlife. Following the construction of a causeway, this is a major entry point to the Dava Way. The buffer at the end of the railway siding has been

The restored buffer at Laurels Bridge.

restored, and the wall of the siding itself is clearly visible. When the railway opened, this was a major loading point for the bulk transport of cattle and sheep. Previously, cattle from throughout the Highlands had been driven by drovers all the way to their destination markets (see p. 162). The ending of droving reduced travel times from a week or more to a single day. Loads of sheep were carried northwards from the Lowlands in spring to benefit from the summer grazing, then returned in autumn for fattening up and butchering. As a consequence the area round the platform was refreshed continuously with animal dung, hence the luxurious growth of nettles to this day.

Mimulus and water forget-me-not are prominent in the Breathing Place in summer. In the pond there, look out for bulrushes, scrophularia and greater spearwort. In the birchwood beyond the pond are large clumps of *Gaultheria shallon*, a shrub in the heather family, imported from North America. Resident treecreepers in the wood race up and down the tree trunks. There are a dozen or so numbered bird boxes for blue and great tits scattered around the Breathing Place area, which can have their lids lifted carefully for a brief peep and replaced.

WAYPOINT 4 (NJ019501)
Peathillock

The cutting here rapidly became a swamp when the railway was abandoned in 1968 and there were no longer railwaymen to maintain the drains. In 2011, with funding help from Paths for All, the Dava Way Association unblocked the drains and stripped the surface of organic material to create the firm dry path which walkers currently enjoy. The exposed ceramic drains, which probably date back to 1863, can be clearly seen on the east side of the track.

Beyond Peathillock the view opens up as the path goes along an embankment which divides the fields of the farms to the west, Presley, Muir of Logie and Drumine. Traffic on the A940 comes into view again across the fields to the west before a short stretch of woodland leads to . . .

WAYPOINT 3 (NJ031524)
Clashdhu Road Crossing

The construction of the railway involved hundreds of navvies from far afield and their camps must have been spread over the wide farmland area you have just crossed (see the History of the Highland Railway over Dava on p. 193).

Southbound train approaching Dunphail.

The Altyre Burn crossing being put into place.

Another change of landscape takes you through more woodland with exposed outcrops which illustrate the effort which was required to create the railway. After a mile a metal bridge crosses the Altyre Burn. This was generously gifted by AJ Engineering, Forres, to replace the railway bridge which had been dismantled in 1968, and the piers of which are still visible. The new bridge was installed in 2004 and was an essential link in completing and opening the Dava Way.

Shortly beyond it lies . . .

WAYPOINT 2 (NJ043536)
Scurrypool Bridge

This turreted bridge in Scottish Baronial style mirrors the one at Lady Catherine's Halt near Grantown (see Waypoint 18, p. 122). The directors of the Inverness and Perth Junction Railway (shortly to become the Highland Railway) wanted their new railway to combine function with fine architecture. It was described as 'the romantic Scurrypool Bridge' on the first safety inspection journey of the new railway on 31 July 1863. The first public train

Ramp leading to the crossing over Squirrelneuk Bridge.

ran here on 3 August 1863, with the journey from Forres to Aviemore (36 miles) taking one and a half hours, not all at a uniform speed! The full extent of the bridge is not immediately apparent, and it is worth descending to the stream to appreciate how long it is.

A rather plainer bridge 100 yards to the north with a ramp on the south side leading to the road over the railway is called Squirrelneuk Bridge, and is the next feature on the route.

The path continues up a hill and into woodland to avoid a damp and undrained deep cutting. From a wooden bench there is a view of nearby Gallows Hill, a place of summary justice administered in the sixteenth and seventeenth centuries by the lairds of Altyre, who could, and on one occasion did, sentence someone to hanging as the penalty for what might seem to us the relatively minor offence of stealing a cheese! In the far distance the hills of Sutherland can be observed in fine weather. The path gains further height before reaching a fork, and here take care to follow the waymarkers and ignore a forestry road branching off to the right leading past a cottage. The path continues through woodland until eventually it emerges onto the largest embankment on the entire Dava railway, from which there are fine views to the east, including the tower of Rafford Church, built in 1824 to the design of the prolific Edinburgh architect James Gillespie Graham. The village of Rafford had a wooden station platform, but the traffic was so light that in 1865 it was dismantled and rebuilt at Aberfeldy. Nothing now remains of the site of this station, which lay just north of the present bridge over a minor public road. More woodland follows, predominantly Scots pine, at the end of which a wide bridge crosses the Mosset Burn at a diagonal angle in such a way that that the burn can easily be passed unnoticed. You then come to an area of open farmland to the east – notice on the left of the track an earthwork, which is a bund established as part of the Forres flood protection scheme completed in 2009. In the event of extreme weather conditions the farmland to your right becomes flooded and the floodwater is contained in Chapelton Dam which lies in the far distance. The path then descends gently as you come to . . .

WAYPOINT 1 (NJ037566)
Dallas Dhu Distillery

Dallas Dhu is described in the section on the history of whisky (see p. 182). The noticeboard at the distillery gives charges and opening times. From here it is a mile walk down the former railway track to the end of the Dava Way in Mannachie Avenue, from where waymarkers guide you through playing fields and the grounds of Forres Academy, then through residential streets back to the centre of Forres.

Your circuit of the Moray Way is now complete!

4
OTHER LONGER ROUTES IN AND AROUND MORAY

The Speyside Way
Grantown to Newtonmore

The southern section of the Speyside Way originally terminated at Aviemore, then in 2015 it was formally extended to Newtonmore. This extension passes through the most tourist-intensive and history-rich part of the Speyside Way and falls naturally into six contrasting subsections averaging roughly six miles each, and defined by seven towns and villages. The very broad descriptions of these sub-sections are:

Grantown–Nethybridge	5 miles/8km; farmland.
Nethybridge–Boat of Garten	6 miles/10km; conifers.
Boat of Garten–Aviemore	6 miles/10km; the Strathspey Railway.
Aviemore–Kincraig	8 miles/13km; birchwood.
Kincraig–Kingussie	7 miles/12km; flood-plain.
Kingussie–Newtonmore	3 miles/5km; farmland.

All of these subsections follow railway lines, either past or present, and have motor roads close by which offer good possibilities for covering parts of the way at different times. The Speyside Way is sufficiently well waymarked that few detailed instructions are required to follow its course. All except Grantown–Nethybridge are fully cycleable. The following notes cover only some of the highlights: full route details and maps can be found in the 2021 edition of the Rucksack Reader guide to the Speyside Way referenced on p. 8. Harveys' map of the Speyside Way also covers the full route from Newtonmore to Buckie.

Accommodation to suit all budgets is reasonably plentiful. In 2021 Stagecoach bus route 34X served Grantown, Nethybridge, Boat of Garten and Aviemore at a frequency of around ten journeys a day in each direction at the summer peak. Service 32 operated between Aviemore and Newtonmore at roughly half this frequency. Aviemore is a main station on the Perth–Inverness line, and is also served by frequent express coaches operating between Inverness and Perth, Glasgow and Edinburgh. For more information go to *www. travelinescotland.com.*

Grantown–Nethybridge

If you wish to abandon the Moray Way near Grantown in order to continue on the Speyside Way, leave the former at the east side of the old Spey Bridge (see p. 114) and proceed down a tarmac road with prominent signs for the Grantown East Heritage Centre on your left. Cross the A95 and, with the Grantown Smokehouse on your right, look for a waymarker pointing to a footpath which marks the start of the track to Nethybridge. At Balliefurth the route broadens and then narrows again, passing the ruined Castle Roy and close to it the former Abernethy Church, which has been converted into a community café, wedding venue and mini-museum – a good spot for a break, but it is only open at selected times.

Nethybridge–Boat of Garten

When the path reaches a minor public road, turn left to enter the village and proceed through it to where, at a bend in the B970, a waymarker directs you to tracks through the Abernethy forest, which take you close to the RSPB Osprey Visitor Centre – worth a detour between April and August when the ospreys are resident. The Speyside Way continues along a footpath running alongside the public motor road to the Centre. When the B970 is reached, follow it to Boat of Garten, where the Strathspey Railway station is the highlight.

Boat of Garten–Aviemore

The Speyside Way follows National Cycle Network Route 7 for most of this section and is never too far away from the Strathspey Heritage Railway which runs from Aviemore via Boat of Garten to Broomhill. It is the ambition of its directors to reach Grantown one day. The route passes under both the Strathspey and mainline railways before reaching the outskirts of the tourist centre of Aviemore.

Aviemore–Kincraig

This section goes through what in the early nineteenth century was Gordon country. The whole area is known as Kinrara which was also the name of the Duchess of Gordon's house by the river, and in Victorian times was the preserve of the aristocratic upper classes whose high living is vividly portrayed in *Memoirs of a Highland Lady* by Elizabeth Grant of Rothiemurchus, recently reprinted by Canongate Press. The dramatic contrast between social conditions two centuries ago and now gives food for thought.

Work on the paths here has recently been undertaken with the aim of guaranteeing consistently comfortable walking and cycling. The route passes close to the large Dalraddy caravan park, from which there is a path to the top of Tor Alvie, a fine viewpoint on which stands the monument to the 5th Duke of Gordon, a massive pillar, built around 1840. The Gordon estate here was given to the Duchess of Gordon (d. 1812) as a settlement following divorce from her philandering husband — the very man commemorated in the monument!

A possible detour in the Kincraig area, approached on the secondary public road to Kingussie, is to the Highland Wildlife Park where, among other highlights, wildcats can be seen close-up.

Kincraig–Kingussie

From Kincraig the Speyside Way proceeds to the east of Loch Insh before heading towards the Drumguish birch woods, then continues on a mix of public roads and tracks to Kingussie. On the Way to the west is the major RSPB reserve of Insh Marshes with a car park and signs pointing to the public hides from which huge numbers of birds can be observed in the right seasons. Before you enter Kingussie on the minor public road leading off the B970, it is worth taking a little extra effort to have a walk around Ruthven Barracks, the ruins of the imposing barracks built by the Hanoverian government as part of its plan to tame the Highlands following the 1715 Jacobite rebellion.

Kingussie–Newtonmore

The final section follows the well-surfaced National Cycling Network Route 7 close to the A86, which used to be the main road between the towns before the A9 was constructed. The extensive Highland Folk Museum with its open-air exhibits and reconstructed Pictish village is an outstanding attraction providing a beguiling way of spending an hour or two.

If you think these final miles are a rather tame ending to the Speyside Way, you can take a seven-mile alternative route into the hills and enjoy some fine scenery. Start from the road which leads uphill from the public car park next to the Duke of Gordon Hotel in Kingussie and goes up the valley of the river Gynack, a tributary of the Spey. Just before the golf course look for a path which takes you into the woods, and has reasonable waymarking all the way to Newtonmore, although be careful at a path junction just over a stile to turn right, rather than going up a path to the crags which is a cul-de-sac. If you are still feeling energetic the six-mile Wildcat Trail circumnavigates Newtonmore and gives a good flavour of its wild hinterland.

Kingussie was once noted as a 'health town'. In 1885 a young Swiss doctor, Walter de Watteville, came to Kingussie as a GP. A keen skier, he was impressed by the clean Highland air and, convinced of its potentially beneficial effects for tuberculosis sufferers, he raised funds to build a 27-bed sanatorium. The treatment for tuberculosis included sleeping outside on balconies of the sanatorium even in the depths of winter. On Dr de Watteville's death in 1918 the sanatorium was bought by a French doctor, Dr Savy, who brought with him as nurses nuns of the order of the Sisters of Saint Vincent de Paul which was noted for doing good and charitable work among the poor. In the 1960s as TB cases declined and the nuns grew older, the Sisters changed the sanatorium to an old people's home. When the Sisters' numbers declined further the building was sold and eventually taken over by the NHS in 1986 to be run as a community hospital, a role which, as with the Ian Charles Hospital in Grantown, ended in October 2021 when a new health centre in Aviemore became operational.

The Speyside Way Spur
Ballindalloch to Tomintoul

Although the name implies that this route is attached to the Speyside Way, and hence linked with the Moray Way, it is in reality a detached 15-mile 'there and back' hill-walking route, separated from the Moray Way by a couple of miles of motor road along the B9137, A95 and B9008, and finally a quarter of a mile of unclassified road just beyond the house at Auldich, at the end of which is a small parking area. In marked contrast to the Speyside Way it is a route through the eastern Highlands which traverses moorland and hill country, opening up good views of the Cairngorms and the Cromdale Hills, even though its highest point is only just over 1,700 feet/520 metres. Full route details can be found in both of the Speyside Way guides cited on p. 8.

Historic Routes

There are two routes within the Moray Way circuit which are signposted by Scotways, the Scottish Rights of Way Society. These are the Mannoch Road and the Lone Road. The southern half of a third road, the Via Regia, makes a good, if quite strenuous, circular walk by combining it with part of the Dava Way. A fourth road, the Old Military Road, can also be used to form a circular route with part of the Dava Way.

The Mannoch Road
Elgin to Knockando

This is the oldest direct route from Elgin to the south, having probably been so since the seventeenth century. In the 1680s a young man and his fiancée from Knockando set out to collect the bride's wedding dress in Elgin, but sadly both perished in a winter storm on the way home. The seven-mile route, which is mountain bike passable with only a little difficulty in the half-mile middle section, reaches maximum heights of around 1080 feet (330 metres) and is notable for the fine views which unfold, of the Moray Firth and distant Sutherland hills if travelling south to north, or of the Spey valley if travelling north to south.

Cars can easily be parked at either end. If starting from the north at Bardonside (NJ212542), broad tracks double as service routes for the Rothes wind farm on Cairn Uish. Take the left-hand track at the bothy where the wind farm traffic goes westward, then at NJ206496 take the right-hand track and follow it for 800 metres until it turns westward at NJ202489. Look for a much smaller track doubling back at first and leading through the woods to emerge at NJ202484. From here it is necessary to negotiate 400 metres or so over a peat bog which is regularly very damp underfoot, while heading for the end of the southern vehicle track at NJ202481. Wayfinding from the south is easier, since from the end of the vehicle track the gap in the forest at NJ202484 is easily detected and the route from there on is obvious. OS Landranger sheet 28 (Elgin, Dufftown and surrounding area) refers.

The Lone Road

This seven-mile/11km Heritage Path was probably part of an eighteenth-century cattle droving route. Farming of cattle prospered in Scotland following the 1707 Union, and

Bridge on the Lone Road near Auchness.

grew to a point when by 1750 Scotland exported around 30,000 head of cattle, increasing to 75,000 by the time of the Napoleonic wars. The drovers who brought the cattle south were remarkably hardy men who made their living by a single drover and his dog driving herds of up to fifty beasts at a time. Anecdote has it that while the drovers lingered at their destination to enjoy the fruits of the money received, the dogs were sent off to find their own way home – which they did! The drovers were contracted by farmers from all over northern Scotland to take animals to the cattle markets or 'trysts' in the lowlands, of which Falkirk, Crieff and Callander were the most notable examples. The drovers carried arms such as broadsword, knife and pistol which were exempt from the Disarming Acts which followed the 1745 rebellion. They travelled light, and typically survived on a diet of oatmeal mixed with water, cooked if possible. Cattle were generally shod and nightly pasturage had to be found, which is why the traffic came to be concentrated on a network of drove roads, which dodged bridges where possible in order to avoid having to pay tolls. Droving declined first because landlords disputed rights of passage, and charged for increasingly well-fertilised stances – the drovers were victims of their own success! Secondly, Aberdeen Angus beef became favoured in the Lowlands, reducing the market for cattle from the Highlands. Somewhat later the Lone Road may have been used as a whisky smuggling route.

The starting point going east to west is a road junction at NJ120501 where there is room to park a few cars. Proceed to Auchness farm, beyond which lies a secret valley to the north. The route is easy to follow and is mostly wide enough for vehicles, until the burn crossing at Redcraig (NJ100481), where a bridge has long been down. There are some parts west of here which may be damp after spells of wet weather. There are ruins of former farmsteads to be seen at Park and at the Lone Farm from which the route takes its name. The remains of Lone Farm are on a miniature plateau north of the path, and are easily missed. The turbines of Berry Burn wind farm come into view as the path approaches its western end at Johnstripe. OS

The remains of Park Croft.

Landranger sheets 27 (Nairn and Forres) and 28 (Elgin and Dufftown) cover the route.

Via Regia

This is almost certainly the oldest road linking Moray with the south. It was used by King Alexander II in 1230 when he held his Christmas court at Elgin as a way of demonstrating his authority over the rebellious Mac-William tribe.

Travelling from north to south, cars can be parked at Auchnagallin (*ached conai* = field of the ear of corn, NJ048338). A second Huntly's Cave at NJ045360, fashioned from boulders of a granitic outcrop, is worth scrambling off the track to explore. The route follows the northward course of the Ourack Burn past a ruined croft at Badahad, and after a downhill stretch crosses what can be in spate the formidable *Allt Bog na Fiodhaig* (= burn of the bird cherry) via stepping stones. Shortly afterwards the direction of the track changes from north to west to join the Dava Way just beyond Attendow farmhouse, now used as a store. Looking east at the turning point you will see the remains of what was Ourack Farm on a small plateau on the opposite bank of the burn.

The site of Badahad – only the flue remains.

The northward track continuing from the turning point and shown on the Ordnance Survey map does not exist, though this may change when Vattenfall build a wind farm in this area (see p. 204) with a resulting road complex. The fit and determined may manage to heather-bash a way through boggy ground towards a conifer plantation from which a path leads past the ruin of Lynagowan and onwards on a Land Rover track to the junction of the Ourack and the River Divie, over which there is a ford at NJ047423. This is another formidable obstacle for walkers even when the Divie is relatively low, but it can be circumvented by following a barely discernible footpath on the west bank of the Divie until the Bridge of Feakirk is reached. The route for those who choose to cross the ford passes the ruined croft of Glenmore, with another deserted croft, Shenvault, visible to the east, then reaches the somewhat modest Falls of Feakirk and eventually the Bridge of Newton, where there is a small car parking area at the end of a motor road to Dunphail, via the hump-backed Bridge of Bantrach. This is where walkers should park if intending to explore the Via Regia from south to north.

It is a matter of wonder how Alexander II and his court retinue managed to make a winter journey on this route nearly nine hundred years ago.

The Old Military Road

Following the 1715 rebellion, the Hanoverian government set about constructing a network of roads as part of its policy of taming the Highlands, a project which continued after the 1745 rebellion. It is possible to savour some of this network within Moray.

Major Caulfeild, General Wade's second-in-command, was responsible for the construction of a road connecting military centres at Blairgowrie and Fort George (Wade himself died in 1748). Part of this road necessarily went through Moray and some remains of it cross Dava Moor. The necessary crossing of the Spey was achieved by the construction of the old Spey Bridge in 1754 by Lord Charles Hay's regiment (see p. 114). The road followed a diagonal course through the as yet unbuilt territory of Grantown, and went on via the lodge of Camerory which lies at the end of a minor public road.

From Camerory, an uphill track leads to the edge of the moor. Traces of the Military Road cease at this point, but it is straightforward to follow a line of fenceposts which lead to the ruined farmhouse of Anabord. A significant crossing of the Anabord Burn is required and there is a long broken-down bridge which would have been helpful for this, but fortunately the burn shrinks rapidly and an upstream diversion to a narrow enough place to cross takes only a little time. From Anabord an estate track leads over a ford and meets the A939 at a point where the Dava Way can be joined. The Old Military Road itself continues northwards from Anabord on a surfaced track to join the A939 at the 'Jesus Saves' stone. This boulder has been there for many years and humourists regularly add comments, 'Jesus saves . . . with the TSB', '. . . his breath to cool his porridge', etc. The stone however has an official custodian nominated by the Baptist Church in Grantown, and the quips are never allowed to persist for long! From this point the Military Road does not reappear until, at NH997391 on the Nairn Road, a secondary Military Road proceeding to Forres can be followed as far as the Dorback Burn, which flows out of Lochindorb. The Dorback is a substantial river, and an effective barrier to completing the final northern mile to its junction with the A940.

The Cromdale Hills Ridge

This is a route whose climax is a four mile ridge walk along the boundaries of Moray, thus looking down on much of the Speyside Way territory in the valley below.

A good circular walk has as its start point the car park situated just off the B9136 at NJ155265. Walk along the minor public road to Milton (NJ140248), then follow a track to grouse butts which continues uphill. When this peters

The Jubilee Cairn – the summit of the Cromdale Hills.

out, the rest of the way is clear to the highest point at the Jubilee Cairn on *Creagan a' Chaise*, which lies on the Moray/Cairngorm National Park boundary. The four-mile walk along the ridge leads to the second summit *Carn a Ghille Chearr*, the highest peak completely within Moray. In early summer the moorland is brightened by swathes of white cloudberries which turn into orange, and then with red berries later in the year. Proceed down to Lyne (NJ161283) and follow the track alongside the River Avon to return to the car park.

The Isla Way
Keith to Dufftown

Although outside the bounds of the Moray Way, the Isla Way is another relatively low-level route within Moray which has an appeal similar to that of the Moray Way. The Isla Way is a family-friendly cycle trail and walking path that uses a mixture of woodland trails, minor tarmac roads and field paths, taking in a considerable variety of scenery along its length. The 13-mile/20km route links

167

the world's malt whisky capital, Dufftown, to the market town of Keith by running for part of its way through the picturesque Isla Valley. The route follows quite closely the line of the Keith to Dufftown Heritage Railway, which means that with careful timing a return to the start point is possible, either on foot or bicycle.

Features include a couple of castles, eleven distilleries, an ancient kirk, an adventure centre, a water-powered mill and a suspension bridge crossing. The trail is well signed between Dufftown and Drummuir using the Isla Way logo. From Drummuir to Keith it mostly follows quiet public roads with a mile-long section along the B9014 before signing is resumed.

Start Points: The official start/finish points are Reidhaven Square in Keith and the Old Clock Tower in Dufftown, site of the tourist information centre. However, by using the Keith and Dufftown Railway (KDR) you can have a mid entry point at either Drummuir Station or Towiemore Halt, allowing you to cycle or walk the trail back to your starting point.

Keith Start Point: From Reidhaven Square where the no. 10 bus stops, head uphill towards the domed St Thomas Chapel and continue along Chapel Street, crossing Land Street, and coming to a T-junction. Take a left onto Cameron Drive, and then fork right onto Braeside and head for the trees. You are now on the Isla Way.

Dufftown Start Point: From the old clock tower head for Mortlach and Rhynie. As you drop down the hill look for the signs with the Isla Way logo on your left, opposite the entrance to Mortlach Church.

5
WHISKY and DISTILLERIES
The History of Distilling

The earliest written records of the distillation of alcohol appear in Italy in the thirteenth century. Techniques for doing so spread through medieval monasteries, where alcohol was used largely for medicinal purposes, internally as an anaesthetic, externally as an antibiotic, and also in the treatment of colic and smallpox. Distilling techniques were brought to Ireland and Scotland at around this time by monks travelling north from warm countries on the continent to establish new monasteries. Irish annals record the death in 1405 of a royal heir 'after drinking whiskey – the *uisce beatha* [sic] or water of life'. The annalist goes on to say that it proved to be ***uisce marbhta***, the water of death! Yet another such casualty was reported in 1463. Since wine could not easily be produced in northern climates, barley beer was distilled into a liquor which became whisky. The practice of medicinal distillation eventually passed from a monastic setting to the secular world via professional medical practitioners of the time such as the Guild of Barber Surgeons.

By following the history of the various Speyside distilleries, it is possible to trace how the whisky industry evolved from hundreds of tiny illegal distilling operations in the hills, and after the making of it was legalised, there was a period of entrepreneurship with distilling usually done by single individuals or families. This evolved in turn through mergers into a number of bigger units, which have been taken over in recent years by large, often international, concerns. The highlighted parts of this section indicate the main developments in the whisky industry prior to the twentieth century.

1494: The name 'whisky' first appeared in the Scottish Exchequer Rolls when one Friar Cor received an order from King James IV for what would today be about 500 bottles. Meanwhile Speyside farmers had discovered the art of making whisky using their surplus barley during the quieter winter months.

1625: A malt tax which infuriated Scots in general was levied, and thereafter the first Scottish Excise Act was introduced in 1644. This was then followed by the imposition of an import duty of a crown per gallon thanks to increasing demand from England. These moves started a long and violent struggle between small-scale distillers and the royal excisemen or 'gaugers' that was to continue for nearly 200 years. Smuggling became commonplace and illicit distilling flourished. Thousands of clandestine stills were hidden in the glens, while smugglers and villagers worked out secret codes by which warnings and and methods of transporting the whisky were signalled. In the age before rapid communication, whisky served as a local currency. Even church ministers were involved in its storage and transportation — accounts books show that the parish minister of Cromdale was the best customer for Balmenach whisky, surpassing even the laird and doctor.

From around 1750 whisky was a commodity enjoyed by all classes of society, being drunk at all times of day from breakfast onwards, and by all ages from small children upwards. The remoteness of Speyside made it a prime centre for smuggling and illicit distilling.

1797: An Act of Parliament divided Scotland into Highlands and Lowlands. In the latter, duty was charged by the gallon, while in the former by the size of the still. Resentment in the Highlands was further increased by an Act of 1814 that made stills of less than 500 gallons illegal. 500 gallons was more than enough to use up all the disposable barley grown in the Highlands, so there could only be a few legal distilleries, thus ruling out farmers' sales of any surplus barley and further incentivising illicit spirits. In an attempt at fairness a further Act of 1816 reduced the 500 gallon limit to 40; nevertheless, by the 1820s, as many as 14,000 illicit stills were being reported and confiscated every year, and more than half the whisky consumed in Scotland was being enjoyed without payment of duty.

In the days of the illicit stills, even the landless with the means to equip themselves with distilling equipment could enter into the trade, sending their uncoloured whisky south in barrels hung over the backs of strings of ponies, using hill tracks and roads rather in the manner of the cattle drovers a generation earlier. It was a practice which allowed many crofters to supplement their pitiful income from the crofts. It was not until after whisky production was legalised that distillers began to recognise that the type of wooden container in which spirit is stored is a significant element in the colour and taste of the final product. Towards the end of the smuggling times, technical developments, the increasing availability of metal, particularly copper, and the skills to work it, resulted in crudely wrought stills becoming widely available. However, distillation was usually carried out on a very small scale, often in private domestic stills. Production methods were crude, and the quality of spirit variable. Much was distilled from a mash of malt, but in some places grain and malt were mixed together, in others oats were used. In times of scarcity distillers would simply use whatever raw material was to hand. Often spirits were drunk mixed with aromatics, milk or fruit, not just for recreational purposes, but to cure a variety of illnesses and maladies. This was not whisky as we know it, rather it was the liquid named in Gaelic *uisge beatha*, water of life.

The continued flouting of the law eventually prompted the Duke of Gordon of Gordon Castle, on whose extensive lands some of the finest illicit whisky in Scotland was being produced, to propose in the House of Lords that the Government should make it profitable to produce whisky legally.

The earliest established and named Scotch whisky was the Glenlivet, until 1823 produced by George Smith in locations hidden away from the Customs Officers and soldiers amongst the hills and abundant springs. Its fame spread so fast that during a ceremonial visit to Scotland in 1822, King George IV asked to try a drop of what had become the famous, if doubtfully legal, Glenlivet whisky.

1823: A more moderate Excise Act allowed the small-scale distilling of whisky upon payment of a licence fee of £10, and a set payment per gallon of proof spirit produced. This caused a decline in smuggling, and paved the way for the creation of the modern distilling industry. By 1830 smuggling had all but ceased, but the expertise acquired in distilling illicitly was to lead to Speyside becoming established as the heart of the Scottish whisky industry. Many of the present-day distilleries stand on sites used by the smugglers over two centuries ago.

From around 1830 whiskies began to be stored and matured in wooden barrels from which they took their colour. As wood is a natural product, each tree species is different and imparts different flavours and colours to the whisky during maturation. One of the skills of whisky makers is in ensuring that colour is as consistent as possible from one bottling to another. The ancient craft of cooperage, that is making wooden casks or barrels, began to be used around this period as an essential subsidiary element in whisky manufacture and maturing. Large distilleries began to appear, of which the major ones are described below in chronological order of opening. Until the early 1960s virtually no malt whisky went outside Scotland, and drinkers in the USA in particular were sceptical about buying whisky from a single distillery. Now single malts are prized as the apex of the luxury whisky market. Speyside is one of Scotland's five malt whisky areas and contains approximately a quarter of the country's 76 or so active distilleries, the other areas being Highland, accounting for over half, Lowland, Campbeltown and Islay.

The following is a list of Speyside distilleries in chronological order. To give an idea of relative sizes the figure following the distillery name is the annual capacity (as opposed to current production) in millions of litres. Specialists seeking more information should consult the *Malt Whisky Year Book* (*www. maltwhiskyyearbook.com*) which contains a huge wealth of detail concerning all malt whisky distilleries, both in Scotland and throughout the world.

1823: **Mortlach** (3.8) distillery, now owned by the multinational company Diageo, was founded by James Findlater. It was built around a well previously used for illicit whisky. It was substantially upgraded in 2014. Its product's rich and powerful flavours have led to its nickname 'The Beast of Dufftown'.

1824: **Glenlivet** (21.0) distillery was formally and legally opened. Glenlivet continued to operate during the Second World War, but with reduced manpower and rationed raw materials, so that while it continued to earn US dollars as an export, previously laid-down stocks shrank and warehouses were emptied to meet demand. In 1978 Glenlivet ceased to be a family business on being taken over by Seagram, who thus acquired five of the major Speyside distilleries. It is now owned by Pernod Ricard, who also own Chivas Royal, for whom Glenlivet is one of its four high-prestige brands. 250 bottles from whisky distilled at Glenlivet and casked by Gordon & Macphail in 1940 were released in September 2021, making this 80-year-old the longest-matured whisky in the world. Profits from the resulting sales are earmarked for the 'Trees for Life' charity which aims to restore parts of the ancient Caledonian forest.

1824: **The Macallan** (15.0) distillery was one of the first to be legally licensed. It was founded by Alexander Reid, a barley farmer and schoolteacher. The original name of the area was 'Maghellan', taken from the Gaelic word *magh*, meaning fertile ground, and *Ellan*, from the monk St Fillan who had a close association with the church that stood in the grounds of the Macallan estate until 1400. The original distillery was founded by William

Robertson whose family acquired Highland Distillers in 1887. William's granddaughters inherited the business, and at the same time established the Robertson Trust, a charity which distributes the dividends of the company in grants to deserving causes throughout Scotland. The Macallan distillery belongs to the Glasgow-based Edrington group who also own the Highland Park and Famous Grouse brands, as well as Glen Rothes distillery which it bought from Berry Bros & Rudd in 2017. The Macallan estate extends to 458 acres which are managed for farming, wildlife conservation and the cultivation of a unique variety of barley. Macallan whiskies have come to dominate the league of whisky values. In 2019 a 1926 bottle fetched a then record £1.5 million at auction.

1824: Cardhu (3.4), called Cardow until 1981, was licensed by John Cumming and operated by him and his wife Helen. John received three convictions for illegal distilling, but the fact that they were still able to continue suggests that the local magistracy was prepared to turn a blind eye to it for much of the time. Helen sold bottles of whisky to passers-by through the window of their farmhouse, and also made long treks to Elgin along the Mannoch Road (see p. 161) to sell it there. Because of their location on a hillside, Helen could see the excisemen and police coming and would throw flour on herself to disguise the smell of whisky so that she was able to say that she was baking bread. She would then offer them tea, meanwhile flying a flag outside which the other nearby distilleries could see and take appropriate action.

Cardhu started as a farm distillery working on a seasonal basis after the harvest had been gathered. In 1885 the distillery was rebuilt on a new piece of land but continued to stay in the hands of the Cummings, and was run by their daughter-in-law Elizabeth Cumming. The stills from the old distillery building were sold to William Grant, who set up Glenfiddich Distillery in 1886. The new building and stills allowed production to be tripled, and in 1893 Elizabeth Cumming sold the distillery to Johnnie

Walker and Sons, although the Cumming family continued to be involved in its day-to-day running. Cardhu Distillery has worked continuously since then apart from a break due to the onset of the Second World War.

In 1960 the distillery's still-house, mash-house and tun-room were rebuilt, and in 1970 steam-coils were introduced to heat the six stills, allowing them to run slowly while remaining hot. Spring water from Mannoch Hill started to be mixed with water from the local Lynne Burn to supply the increased production of the distillery. Cardhu remains part of the Johnnie Walker group, and contributes to its blends.

1824: **Balmenach** (2.8) near Cromdale was founded by a Macgregor family of two brothers and a sister from Tomintoul, who came over the hills, initially to farm, but they soon found that selling whisky made from their surplus barley was a more profitable line. After the 1823 Act, following sound advice from the local preventative officer (aka gauger), Balmenach became one of the earliest distilleries to be licensed. The Macgregor family were stern Presbyterians who, having fallen out with the powers that be in the established church, founded the Free Church in Cromdale. This is now the village hall, and offers refreshments daily during the summer months. Successive generations of the Macgregor family continued to run the distillery until in 1897 it was formed into a limited liability company, which after a few years was taken over by Distillers Company Limited. Balmenach continued production until the 1990s, when it was mothballed by its then owners, Diageo. In 1997 Diageo sold it to Airdrie-based Inver House Distillers who distil gin there under the name *Caorunn*.

1826: **Aberlour** (3.8) was one of the earliest and more attractive and traditional-looking distilleries on Speyside, and occupied the site of what is now Walker's factory. It was demolished in 1879 but it is not clear when it ceased production.

Glen Grant gardens.

1840: **Glen Grant** (6.2). Grant is the surname of the two brothers, farmer's sons, who founded the distillery, the first in the village of Rothes where, with no other industry to compete, an eager source of labour was on the doorstep. Before the coming of the Morayshire railways to Speyside, Garmouth was the principal seaport for the Spey valley, through which coal and other cargoes were imported. The extension of the Morayshire railway to Rothes in 1858 prompted an expansion of Glen Grant in 1861from around 160,000 litres per year to nearly 800,000 litres in 1888. James, the younger brother, seems to have been an astute businessman. It is said that when transacting business with neighbouring farmers he would produce a hundred-pound bank note to pay them, knowing that the country people would be unable to give change for that amount, and thereby giving him extended credit! Uniquely among Speyside distilleries, James Grant's mansion house had a fine garden in a steeply rising valley, with a small safe embedded in the rocks, from which he delighted his visitors by pouring them a dram. The gardens, once employing fifteen gardeners, can still be visited today.

In 1978 Glen Grant was taken over by the Seagram Company and thus became one of the several Speyside distilleries which was no longer being run as a family concern. The annual production of the distillery at that time was 5.2 million litres, and Seagram immediately set an ambitious modernisation programme in motion. Glen Grant is currently owned by Campari.

1852: **Dailuaine** (5.2) was founded in 1852 by William Mackenzie. It was renovated and enlarged in 1884. In 1891 Dailuaine-Glenlivet Distillery Ltd. was founded, and in 1898, a further merger created Dailuaine-Talisker Distilleries Ltd. In 1915 the company was sold to John Dewar and Sons, and a year later to John Walker and Sons and James Buchanan and Co. In 1917 a fire destroyed the pagoda-style roof, closing the distillery for three years. In 1925 it was bought by the Distillers Company Limited, which renovated it completely in 1960. In 1987 Dailuaine was taken over by United Distillers, now Diageo.

1869: **Cragganmore** (2.2) is also currently owned by Diageo who produce brands such as White Horse and the Claymore. It was founded by John Smith on land leased

Old Cragganmore.

Cragganmore as it is today.

from Sir George Macpherson-Grant, whose family's ancestral home is nearby at Ballindalloch Castle.

Smith was an experienced distiller, and had previously been manager of the Macallan, Glenlivet, and Glenfarclas distilleries. The Cragganmore site was chosen to be close to the then recently opened Strathspey Railway. John Smith was a very portly man and it is reported that he was too broad to get through the passenger carriage doors and thus had to travel in the guard's van. Remains of the original distillery are still to be seen, heavily propped up. The second distillation still at the present distillery has an unusual flat top. Like Cardhu, Cragganmore is part of the Johnnie Walker group, and contributes to their blends.

In **1872** Scotland experienced its first whisky boom. The annual consumption of spirits in Scotland at the time was 23 pints per head, in England 7, and rising. In 1887 there were 129 distilleries in Scotland, 28 in Ireland and 4 in England.

1878: **Glen Spey** (1.4) distillery was built in 1878 by James Stuart, a corn merchant. It was originally an oatmeal mill which was sold to the Gilbey Company of London in 1887. It expanded production capacity from two to four stills in 1970. It uses condensers known as purifiers which produce a lighter spirit, currently used for blending in J&B products. It is now part of the Diageo group of distilleries.

A spot of luck around this time helped whisky's global expansion. In the 1880s, the *phylloxera* beetle devastated French vineyards, and within a few years, wine and brandy had virtually disappeared from cellars everywhere. Canny Scots were quick to take advantage, and by the time the French industry recovered, Scotch whisky had replaced brandy as the spirit of choice for most people.

1879: **Aberlour** (3.8), the second distillery of this name after the first was demolished, was built by James Fleming, son of a local tenant farmer, and designed by the celebrated distillery architect Charles Doig. Fleming died aged 65 in 1895 and is buried opposite the distillery in the village cemetery. Robert Thorne and Sons Ltd then bought the distillery, shortly after which a fire, in 1898, caused a major rebuild. In 1921 the Thornes sold it to W. H. Holt and Sons, then brewers based near Manchester. In 1945 S. Campbell and Sons Ltd. bought the distillery. In 1975 Pernod Ricard acquired Campbell Distilleries, and they joined with Chivas Brothers (Pernod Ricard) in 2001 to form a portfolio of fifteen single malt distilleries and one grain distillery in Scotland, and two gin distilleries in England. In 2002 a new modernised visitor centre was opened.

1879: **Glen Rothes** (5.6) is on a site split in two by the Burn of Rothes, with production on one side and the filling store and warehouses on the other. It is accessed by turning up Burnside Road at a junction close to the traffic lights on Rothes Bridge. It is currently part of the Edrington Group (see under Macallan above).

1886: **Glenfiddich** (13.7) distillery was founded by William Grant in Dufftown. In the 1920s, with prohibition in force in the USA, Glenfiddich was one of a very small number of distilleries to increase production. In the 1950s, the Grant family built up an onsite infrastructure that included coppersmiths to maintain the copper stills, and a dedicated cooperage that is now one of the very few remaining in Speyside distilleries. Following difficult times in the 1960s and 70s, many small, independent distillers were bought up or went out of business; however W. Grant and Sons remained independent. Production was increased and in 1969 the Grants created the first public visitor centre which remains one of the largest and most comprehensive of its kind on Speyside. In this period they also began marketing single malt as a premium brand in its own right, effectively creating the modern single malt whisky category in which Glenfiddich is one of the world's best known names, characterised by its triangular cross-sectioned bottles.

In 1996 sales exceeded 800,000 cases, making Glenfiddich the world's biggest-selling malt whisky, and the Grant family one of the richest families in the UK, noted for philanthropy in supporting the National Piping Centre in Glasgow, the National Museum of Scotland in Edinburgh, the Museum of Flight in East Lothian and the Gordon Highlanders' Museum in Aberdeen. Glenfiddich is managed by succeeding generations of William Grant's descendants who, in September 2014, acquired Drambuie for an undisclosed price, rumoured to be in the region of £100 million.

1892: **Balvenie** (7.0) was founded by William Grant, a farmer's son from Dufftown. Following twenty years, first as a bookkeeper and then manager at Mortlach Distillery, he bought land near Balvenie Castle, and in 1892 work began to convert an eighteenth-century mansion, Balvenie New House, into a distillery which began production in 1893. Grant remained active in the company until his death in 1923 at the age of 83. It is one of the few Scottish distilleries to boast in-house floor-malting, using locally hand-cut peat. These floor-maltings also supply neighbouring Glenfiddich. In 1990 the Grant family extended their site by adding Kininvie Distillery.

1895: **Dufftown** (6.0) distillery, now owned by Diageo, was founded by two Liverpudlian engineers and developed out of a meal mill located by the Dullan Water. Its water source in the Conval Hills is the so-called 'Jock's Well'. Much of its output has a unique bottle shaped like a hip flask, and it is home to the Singleton brand, another component of Johnnie Walker.

1896: **Tamdhu** (4.0) was founded by a group of whisky entrepreneurs who secured a first precious shipment of sherry casks from the finest bodegas in Spain. Tamdhu still matures its whisky in rare and expensive Oloroso sherry casks. A short while after opening ownership was passed on to Highland Distillers. It remained dormant between 1927 and 1947, but came to life again in the early 70s. Its output is an important component of the Famous Grouse, J&B and Cutty Sark blends. Unlike most Speyside distilleries it has no pagoda-shaped roof above the furnaces. In 2010 the Edrington Group, of which Highland Distilleries was by then a subsidiary, closed Tamdhu, moving some of its employees to nearby Macallan. In 2011 it was sold to Ian Macleod Distillers of Broxburn, who reopened it with a series of limited edition bottlings.

1897: **The Imperial** distillery, founded to mark Queen Victoria's Diamond Jubilee, was a producer of single malt Scotch whisky located in Carron, that operated sporadically between 1897 and 1998. Imperial was mothballed and reopened several times in its hundred-year history. The only recent official bottling was a 15-year expression (technical term for the release and promotion of a homogeneous batch), released in the mid 1990s. The distillery was demolished in 2013, and a new distillery, Dalmunach (see p. 185), was established on the site in 2015. The Imperial warehouses survive and remain in use.

1897: **Glendullan** (5.0) distillery in Glen Fiddich was founded by William Williams and Sons, and is now owned by Diageo. It was reputed to be Edward VII's favourite whisky, for which he is known to have placed orders. The site is home to a bio-power plant which processes the liquid co-products from Dufftown and Mortlach distilleries in an anaerobic digestion process which produces bio-gas for its own power.

1898: **Dallas Dhu**, originally named Dallasmore, was built in 1898-9 on a Forres estate called Sanquhar, owned by Alexander Edward. It was designed by Charles Doig, regarded as the doyen of distillery designers, and produced Wright and Greig's popular whisky brand called Roderick Dhu. Production ceased in 1916 due to the First World War. It was sold to J.P.O'Brien in 1919. During the Second World War, in 1940, it closed again. It reopened in 1947 as the whisky industry stepped up exports to boost the economy, but closed again in 1983, at which point it came into the guardianship of Historic Environment Scotland, who run it as an all-the-year-round museum, and may one day bring it back into production.

1898: **Knockando** (1.4) distillery was built by John Tytler Thomson in 1898. In 1904 the distillery was purchased by W. and A. Gilbey, the London gin producer, becoming in the 1960s and 1970s part of J&B/Grand Metropolitan, which is now owned by Diageo. Knockando was the first distillery in Scotland to be built with electric lighting. In 1905 it was linked directly to the Great North of Scotland Railway, which thereby connected it to the main towns of Scotland. Cottages for distillery workers were built nearby, as well as a house for the Customs and Excise Officer. The distillery currently lies near the disused Dalbeallie Station, which is closer to the Tamdhu distillery. The railway has long since been dismantled, and now forms part of the Speyside Way. The old station has been renamed Tamdhu, as the buildings are used by the distillery for meetings. Tamdhu the station was never named as such in railway timetables.

1898: **Benromach** (0.7) distillery just outside Forres is currently owned by Gordon and MacPhail, whisky bottlers

Benromach distillery.

and specialists, whose headquarters are in Elgin. They purchased it in 1993 from United Distillers after it had been mothballed for ten years. The reopening was marked with the release of a 17-year-old celebratory malt, with the first bottles being released in 2004. In 1999 a visitor centre was opened but it closed in 2021. Up until 1931 when it was first mothballed due to the Great Depression it had multiple owners, and changed hands several times. In 1909 its name was changed to Forres Distillery. It reopened in 1937 after which it was sold in 1938 to the National Distillers of America. In 1958 it came back into British hands on its purchase by Distillers Company Limited, which was then a branch of Grand Metropolitan. In 1966 it was refurbished and in 1968 the malting floor was closed. In 1983 it was again mothballed. It has a distinctive red chimney but no pagoda roof. It is the smallest working distillery in Speyside, with a current output of around 400,000 litres per year.

1898: **Glen Elgin** (2.7) distillery lies three miles south of Elgin on the road to Rothes. Its architect was Charles Doig, who accurately predicted that it would be the last distillery built in Speyside for fifty years. Its first owners were William Simpson, a former manager of Glenfarclas, and James Carle, an agent for the North of Scotland Bank. They saw their investment of £13,000 plummet to £4,000 when they sold the distillery in 1901. The original site was chosen for its water source and close proximity to the railway line. Unfortunately the water source proved unreliable, and permission for a railway siding was refused. The distillery soldiered on through several other owners before becoming part of Distillers Company Limited in the 1930s. It was then licensed to White Horse Distillers Ltd. Until the 1950s the distillery and all its equipment were operated and lit by paraffin. Its current owners are Diageo, and its whisky is a key component of White Horse blended whisky, which is exported to over 200 countries worldwide.

1947: The Speyside Cooperage company was founded by the Taylor family, and is the largest independent cooperage in the UK, with branches in Alloa, and also in the USA, in Kentucky and Ohio. In the early 1990s the company outgrew its premises in Craigellachie village and relocated to its present location on the village outskirts. In 2008 Speyside Cooperage was taken over by the group François Frères Tonnellerie.

1960: **Tormore** (4.8), near Advie, was designed by Sir Albert Richardson and is now owned by Chivas Brothers. Until Macallan's new distillery came along, it was unquestionably the most unusual looking distillery in Scotland. Like Macallan, it offers tours. It was founded by Schenley

Water tanks at Roseisle distillery.

Dalmunach distillery.

International who owned the Long John brand which was later sold to Whitbread when it became fashionable for brewing companies to diversify into whisky. A 12-year-old product was launched in 2014 as *The Pearl of Speyside*, after the freshwater pearl mussels to be found in the nearby Spey.

2010: **Roseisle** (12.5) distillery is owned by Diageo, and is the largest Scotch whisky distillery ever built. It covers 3,000 square metres and cost £40 million. In appearance it is quite unlike traditional distilleries, and is more like an industrial chemical site. It is connected by underground pipes to the Burghead malting, thereby providing a water heat exchange to the advantage of both.

2015: **Dalmunach** distillery, which was opened in 2015 by First Minister Nicola Sturgeon on the site of the demolished Imperial Distillery, was designed by the Archial Norr group of architects to recall the previous traditional buildings in a simple yet contemporary way, inspired by the shape of a sheaf of barley. The distillery has distinctive white rendered walls and glass gable walls. There are eight copper pot stills, the tulip-shaped wash stills and onion-shaped spirit stills replicating those used at the old Imperial Distillery. In a departure from distillery tradition, the stills are arranged in a circular pattern to give a feeling of spaciousness. A short distance away the warehouses of the former Imperial Distillery are still standing.

2021-2: **The Cairn** is a new distillery on the A95 at Craggan, just south of Grantown, and is owned by Gordon & MacPhail, their second distillery after Benromach. It is due to go into production in 2023.

The Malt Whisky Trail

This has been set up by a consortium of eight Speyside distilleries, plus the Speyside Cooperage in Craigellachie. Opening hours vary, so they should be phoned or their websites consulted before visiting.

Benromach, Forres: *www.benromach.com*, 01309-675968

Glenfiddich, Dufftown: *www.glenfiddich.com/uk/distillery*, 01340-820373

Cardhu, Knockando: *www.discovering-distilleries/cardhu*, 01479-874635

Speyside Cooperage, Aberlour: *www.speysidecooperage. co.uk*, 01340-871108

Glen Grant, Rothes: *www.glengrant.com*, 01340-832118

Dallas Dhu, Forres (Historic Environment Scotland): *www.historic-environment.scot*, 01309-676548

The remaining distillery in the group, but some way from the Moray Way, is **Strathisla** near Keith. The following distilleries also offer public tours and visitor centres. Expect to pay around £8 per head for a standard tour with tasting, and £100 or even more for more specialised connoisseur tours.

Macallan, Craigellachie: *www.themacallan.com*, 01340-318000

Aberlour: *www.aberlour.com*, 01340-881249

Cragganmore, Ballindalloch: *www.discovering-distilleries/cragganmore*, 01479-874700

Glenfarclas, Ballindalloch: *www.glenfarclas.com*, 01807-500345

Other Moray distilleries some distance from the Moray Way are: Ben Riach, Glenlossie and Mannochmore which share a site, Linkwood, Glen Moray, Longmorn, Speyburn. Of these only Glen Moray operates tours.

Glossary for a Distillery Tour

Raw Material: Traditionally, barley was spread out on the floors of large warm barns, steeped with water, and turned over manually under heat to make it germinate. Nowadays most malt comes from specialised **maltings** such as the one at Burghead. In the distillery it is dried in kilns, often **pagoda**-topped, to halt germination.

Mashing: The malt is crushed to become **grist**, which is a form of starch. Under repeated stirring with water in a **mash tun** it changes into sugar. Successive charges are made progressively warmer until a sugary liquid called **worts** is drawn off, cooled and pumped into **washbacks**, where the residue, **draff**, is a by-product which can be used as cattle food or to produce bio-energy.

Fermentation: Yeast is added to the washbacks and fermentation takes place, typically after 48 hours or so, turning the yeast and sugar into low-strength alcohol, at around 7% by volume (**ABV**). The resulting liquid, called **wash**, is pumped into a **wash charger** from which it is fed by gravity into **wash stills**.

Distilling: Alcohol has a lower boiling point (c. 80 deg) than water, so output from wash stills is vapourised in a **condenser**, a large copper coil, where it becomes **low wines** at about 20% ABV. The residue, **pot ale**, is potential cattle feed. A second distillation takes place in copper stills, heated by either coal fires or steam. Repeated distilling separates the liquid into **foreshot**, **heart** and **feints**. Only the heart is retained for maturation, while feints join the next batch of low wines. By law **Scotch** whisky must have a minimum 40% ABV.

Maturation: The final stage is to feed the spirits into casks which are sealed and stored in **bonded** warehouses. To be designated Scotch, the law requires a minimum of three-year maturation, but usually it is much, much more.

6
RAILWAYS

There are six clearly distinguishable periods in the history of Moray railways:

1. The Morayshire Railway era (1844–1861)

Route: Lossiemouth–Elgin–Orton–Rothes–Dandaleith
(Craigellachie)

On 10 August 1852 the Morayshire Railway company opened the line from Elgin to Lossiemouth after the steam engines had been delivered to Lossiemouth by sea. It was the first railway north of Aberdeen, first promoted in 1844, approved by Act of Parliament and incorporated in 1846. Much of the Elgin to Lossiemouth route is still open as a footpath. In 1858 a second line reached Rothes via Orton by running from a junction with the Inverness and Aberdeen Junction Railway line which had reached Elgin in the same year. This allowed the Morayshire Railway to run through trains from Lossiemouth to Rothes. They then built the line to Rothes via Longmorn, completing this to Dandaleith near Craigellachie in 1863, which made the Orton link redundant. A merger with the Great North of Scotland Railway (GNoSR) was completed in 1861, thereby rescuing the Morayshire Railway from insolvency. The GNoSR's Strathspey line from Keith to Craigellachie and onwards to Abernethy was opened in 1863, the same year in which the Highland Railway (HR) opened their line over Dava.

2. The rail-building era (1863–1923): the Great North of Scotland and Highland Railways

The first station in Forres was built when the Inverness and Aberdeen Joint Railway (I&AJR) extended their railway to Nairn by completing the crossing over the Findhorn,

Carron, a typical station on the Speyside line.

reaching Forres and Elgin in 1858. The Highland Railway grew out of a merger in 1865 between the I&AJR and the Inverness and Perth Junction Railway. The I&AJR opened a line from Inverness to Elgin in 1858 in three stages, building stations in Moray at Forres, Kinloss, Alves, Mosstowie, Elgin, Lhanbryde, Orbliston, Orton, Mulben and Keith. Forres and Elgin are now the only operating stations within the Moray Way area. The Moray Way crosses the existing Inverness to Aberdeen railway at two points, first at Forres and again at Boat o' Brig, where what was then an expensive bridge enabled the I&AJR to extend to Keith, beating its rivals the GNoSR who were reluctant to share the cost of the bridge. Keith thus became the exchange station for journeys from Aberdeen to Inverness.

The GNoSR's line from Keith to Dufftown (now restored as a heritage railway – see p. 168) was opened in 1862, following which the Strathspey line was opened in 1863, the same year in which the I&AJR opened their line over Dava. HR and GNoSR were never good bedfellows, and although they had a common objective in reaching Grantown, they could not agree on a shared site for a station, with the result that Grantown was served by two stations on opposite banks of the Spey, neither of which was central to the town.

The GNoSR stations which opened in 1863 from north to south were:

Craigellachie (called Strathspey Junction until 1864)
Aberlour
Carron
Blacksboat
Ballindalloch
Advie (relocated to a second site in 1868)
Dalvey
Cromdale
Grantown-on-Spey (renamed Grantown-on-Spey
    East by British Rail)
Abernethy (renamed Nethybridge in 1867)

In 1896 when Tamdhu Distillery opened it was provided with a private siding, following which in 1899 a station was built, originally named Dalbeallie (pronounced Dalbee-ally) which was renamed Knockando in 1905. It was later again renamed Tamdhu, and has been restored by Diageo as a meeting-room and conference centre.

The Banff, Portsoy and Strathisla was another small company which had expanded to run trains as far west as Portsoy. It was taken over by the GNoSR who were keen to penetrate the Moray coast, and operated trains to a station they called Fochabers, even although it was four miles from the town. It was later renamed Spey Bay.

1884 saw a race between HR and GNoSR to reach Buckie first, thereby capturing the fish-transporting market there, and filling in the void apparent in the pre-1884 map shown on the next page. Both HR and GNoSR were authorised on the same day, but the HR opened their branch from Keith first, followed shortly by GNoSR's opening of the coast line from Portessie to Elgin via Garmouth. This involved connecting Spey Bay and Garmouth by the viaduct which had taken three years to build, and which is now a hugely important feature of the Moray Way. The GNoSR line survived until the Beeching cuts in 1965, while the HR line was less successful, closing for passenger traffic in 1915 due to the First World War. The rails were lifted in 1917, however they were relaid in phases for the

Moray railways c. 1890.

transport of goods, from Buckie to Portessie in 1919, and from there to Keith in 1923, when the HR became part of LMS. No passenger traffic was reinstated, and in 1937 the second-phase rails were again lifted, except for a short section going north from Keith to Aultmore. Final closure seems to have taken place during the Second World War, certainly no later than 1944.

GNoSR did not open any branch lines in the Moray Way area, although in the 1890s the prospect was raised of a branch line from Ballindalloch to Glenlivet, and possibly onwards to Tomintoul. The motivation for the latter was the discovery of promising iron-ore deposits in the rocks around Tomintoul. Meanwhile in 1862 the HR opened a branch line from Alves to Burghead, with an intermediate station at Wards which occupied a site where the Roseisle Distillery is now located. This line does not appear to have been very successful initially as it was closed in 1863, however it was reopened in 1865. In 1892 the branch line was extended to Hopeman and a new station opened for passengers at Burghead. Before the First World War the line seems to have become popular, transporting timber imports from Norway for the Elgin sawmills and exporting building stone from Cummingston quarry, as well as fish and the products of chemical manure works in Burghead itself.

After the war the goods traffic was greatly reduced, as timber imports from Scandinavia ceased along with the supply of raw material for the chemical works. The fishing industry also declined, and in addition the line suffered from drifting sand which caused blockages, requiring the sand to be shovelled into wagons to clear the line. Freight services to Hopeman ceased in 1957 and the track was up-lifted in 1960. The construction of the Maltings at Burghead led to the track being relaid, and trains continued to run until the early 1990s. The station building itself was burnt down in March 2003, shortly after plans had been put in motion to convert it into a community centre.

As part of the Inverness to Keith line, HR built a station in 1863 which they called Fochabers Town, even although it was a good two miles from Fochabers. Unlike most of HR's stations, which were built of wood, Fochabers Town was built of stone, probably because it served the Duke of Gordon, one of the UK's biggest landowners, at Gordon Castle. The Prince of Wales (later Edward VII) arrived there in the Royal train for a visit in 1900.

In 1893 a branch line to Fochabers was opened and Fochabers Town was renamed Orbliston Junction. A vivid account of the activities of this branch line and the social mores of the late 1920s is given in *Time Does Transfix* by Alfred H. Forbes, published 1997 by the Centre for Scottish Studies, Aberdeen. The author was a junior rail worker at Orbliston who in his later years became Provost of Forres. The arrival of regular bus services from Elgin to Fochabers killed off passenger traffic on the railway, so latterly the line was open only to freight, and it was finally closed in 1966.

Two guards on the Highland Railway were close friends, as were their nephew and son who were to become, respectively, the Prime Minister, James Ramsay Macdonald, and the philanthropist, Sir Alexander Grant, chairman of the biscuit firm McVitie and Price, benefactor of Forres through the gift of the Grant Park, and of Scotland through the foundation of the National Library. More controversial were gifts of 30,000 shares and a Daimler car to the friend of his youth, an early cash for honours scandal!

Whisky and the Railways

Glen Grant was the first to exploit rail conveyance of goods, largely since James Grant, owner of Glen Grant distillery and Provost of Elgin, was a campaigner for and shareholder in the Morayshire Railway.

The arrival of the Speyside railway attracted several distilleries to build close to it: Cragganmore (1869), Tamdhu (1896), Imperial (1897) and Knockando (1898). The last three had private sidings, Cardhu and Cragganmore used public sidings. Cragganmore made history in 1887 when it despatched an entire trainload of whisky to Dundee for blending. Dailuaine and Balmenach built their own lines, the former in 1905, the latter connecting with a siding at Cromdale Station. In 1933 a halt was built on the Speyside railway for the use of Dailuaine's distillery workers.

Legends abound concerning illegal tampering by rail staff with whisky casks in wagons in sidings and awaiting transit in goods sheds. Porters would broach casks and cover the hole with a material which was nearly impossible to detect; more skilful thieves would bore through the floors of wagons to produce a continuous flow!

The History of the Highland Railway over Dava

As early as 1845 a prospectus was issued for a direct railway to connect Perth and Inverness, in competition with an alternative route south via Aberdeen put forward by the Great North of Scotland Railway Company. The direct Highland Railway line was proposed by Joseph Mitchell, a Forres-born civil engineer who had worked

Forres Station in 1898.

under Thomas Telford and became Inspector of Highland Roads and Bridges. Mitchell's original proposal was for a railway from Inverness to Perth via Nairn, from which it proceeded on the route of the A939 to Glenferness, then followed the route of the B9007 to Carrbridge. This route would have involved steep gradients with which steam engines might not have been able to cope, consequently parliamentary approval was not given, and instead the ruling was in favour of reaching Inverness via Aberdeen. In the course of evidence William Austin, a barrister working for the GNoSR, famously ridiculed Joseph Mitchell as being 'the greatest mountain climber ever heard of, who beat Napoleon outright and eclipsed Hannibal'.

Undaunted, Joseph Mitchell persevered with plans for a direct line, and eventually on 22 July 1861 an Act of Parliament for the Inverness and Perth Junction Railway was obtained. Since the Highland Railway's Forres station had been opened in 1858, the prospect of a southern outlet for the goods and produce of the Moray plain was greatly welcomed. On 17 October 1861 a turf-cutting ceremony by the Countess of Seafield for the new line was marked in Forres by a huge parade, amidst a great wave of civic rejoicing.

3 August 1863 was the day of the first public train service between Forres and Aviemore. Not only did local goods and produce have a much shorter journey to

markets in the south, but also the cost of goods such as coal, which had to be imported to the area, fell substantially. Two years prior to the line's opening, and with support from the Earl of Seafield, a new line had been constructed south from Forres and through Grantown, at that time the most populous settlement between Forres and Dunkeld. Amazingly the whole line between Forres and Dunkeld was constructed in a timescale of less than two years, and within two years after that the two railway companies operating east and south of Forres had merged to become the Highland Railway.

It was not only people and businesses at the northern end of the route which stood to benefit from the new rail link. Throughout the eighteenth and early nineteenth centuries, people in Strathspey had looked northwards to the fertile Moray plain and its towns and city as their nearest urban centres. Prior to the railway, harbour improvement at Findhorn in the early nineteenth century ensured that transport by sea was the favoured means for delivering large or valuable cargoes compared with the uncertainties of rough and potentially dangerous roads. The coming of the Dava railway changed all that.

The history and folklore of the line, along with that of parishes such as Edinkillie through which it passed, are described in Section 3 above. The most visible and iconic reminder of past times is the seven-arch Divie Viaduct, 477 feet/145m long, built in 1861 at a cost of around £10,000, and subsequently saved from demolition by the late Lord Laing of Dunphail following the drastic cuts to the British Rail network in 1965 – leaving it now as one of the largest garden ornaments in the country (see also p. 145)!

In the late eighteenth and early nineteenth century, before the arrival of the railway, many men who worked on the land in the fertile Moray plain were forced into unemployment by the pressures of the Agrarian Revolution and the introduction of mechanised farming. Some of them began to scratch out a living in fresh pastures both on Speyside and on what had been the rough moor to the south of Edinkillie. When the railway arrived, the tranquillity of the countryside was disturbed by the coming of the navvies. A tourist of the time described their camps as reminiscent of the Californian gold rush:

> Newly-deposited squatters with their scattering of half-naked imps were lolling around tents and huts with their furniture and utensils half-housed. Booths were spread out on the heather with watches and trinkets glittering in the sun — collections of rubbish designed to mop up the superfluous cash of the monthly payday. On pay-night itself the local inns were full of navvies in various stages of intoxication. When all who did not lodge in the inn were turned out at 11 o'clock, they howled round and round like wolves kept from their destined prey.

The railway construction period thus worked temporary wonders for the local economies of towns like Grantown and Forres, particularly in the local hostelries! Many of the navvies came from Yorkshire — excellent workers, powerfully built and of considerable endurance. Varicose veins were a common complaint of the navvies, caused by extreme muscular pressure from pushing heavy barrows up and down the embankments. Some of the navvies were well-educated, and their ranks included a smattering of down-on-their-luck professional men. Medical needs were met from a sick fund to which all

A Findhorn locomotive.

H.R. Loco 103 makes a nostalgic run in 1965 before taking pride of place in Glasgow's transport museum.

subscribed, although it was reported that many of the prescriptions were for castor oil for their boots!

The Findhorn Railway

In the mid-eighteenth century, Findhorn prospered on maritime trade, exporting timber, fish, grain and potatoes, and importing lime, bone dust and guano, as well as luxury goods sold by Forres merchants. These merchants were alarmed at the prospect that, with the coming of the railways, Findhorn might lose out to Lossiemouth and Burghead (the Moray Railway to Lossiemouth opened in 1845 and the Highland Railway were proposing a branch to Burghead). A Forres solicitor proposed a five-mile branch to connect with a line proposed by GNoSR which would extend their line from Aberdeen through Forres and on to Inverness. A survey was undertaken in 1853 and a Findhorn Railway prospectus was issued. A second survey was made in 1858, by which time I&AJR had reached Forres. In 1859, a Parliamentary bill to authorise the route had an easy passage through Parliament and construction began. In 1860 there were trains on the line running at an average speed of 10 mph. Frequency was later increased to five trains per day, with a special return fare for fishwives to Forres reduced from 8 pence to 6 pence!

In 1862 the Findhorn Railway board handed over the management of the line to I&AJR, who insisted on laying quarry material between the rails so that horses could also be used on it. Another curious novelty which they introduced was a bathing train leaving Forres at 6.30 am and returning by 9 am, to allow workers to have an early morning dip. It never took off!

The line had many problems, both financial and operational, which were not helped by the silting up of Findhorn Bay and the increasing amount of Findhorn traffic which was skimmed off by the new railways from Inverness and Aviemore. The fledgling Highland Railway was not prepared to renew the agreement with the Findhorn Railway, and the line closed in 1869, at which time a timber merchant in Dunphail was the only substantial customer. The rails were lifted in 1873.

3. The LNER and LMS era (1923–1948)

The Highland Railway continued to operate until 1923, when it became part of the London, Midland and Scottish (LMS) Railway. At the same time the Great North of

Poster advertising the Dava line.

Southbound train from Forres in the last days of British Rail.

Scotland Railway became part of the London and North Eastern Railway (LNER). After nationalisation in 1948, both these companies were merged into British Rail which continued services along the Moray lines until the majority were closed in 1965, following the extensive cuts to the British railway network carried out by Beeching.

4. The British Rail era (1948–1996)

Initially British Rail promoted both the Speyside and Dava lines to holidaymakers as the poster on the previous page shows. When problems with the cost of running the lines arose, attempts were made to make the Speyside line viable with a railbus, adding halts at Imperial Cottages, Gilbey's Cottages, Dalvey Farm and Balliefurth Farm. Regular through trains ran from Aviemore to Elgin for the first time, however the railbuses proved unreliable and the service was withdrawn as part of the Beeching cuts. The Speyside and Dava lines were closed to passenger traffic in 1965 and to goods traffic in 1968, although the section from Dufftown to Aberlour remained open for freight until 1971. Although the closures were considered short-sighted and opposed vigorously by many local people at the time, the closure of the line over Dava, rather than the direct Aviemore to Inverness line, has left a legacy in the form of the Dava Way, one of Scotland's Great Trails, the maintenance of which is carried out by volunteers from the Dava Way Association (see pp. 6 and 152).

5. The privatisation era (1996–2022)

After privatisation First Group won the franchise to run Scottish trains. When the franchise came up for renewal, the Dutch company Abellio, competing against National Express, First Group and Virgin Trains, won it and from 1 April 2015 took over all Scottish rail services except the Caledonian Sleeper, which is under contract to be operated by Serco until 2025.

In 2017 Network Rail made major upgrades and improvements costing £1.7M to the Aberdeen–Inverness railway, including straightening the loop which was made in 1863 to carry the line into Forres to accommodate the Dava line, and dualling the line so that trains could pass each other at Forres. The 1965 station was demolished and replaced by the present station, built along modern modular lines. On the line itself shortened HS125 trains which had been transferred from the Great Western route out of Paddington to enhance the rolling stock in Scotland were operating, and rechristened HS7 to reflect the seven Scottish cities which they serve.

6. The nationalisation era (2022–)

Abellio were dogged by strikes over driver-only operating, rolling-stock shortages, and failures to meet punctuality and performance standards. In 2019 the Scottish government announced that Abellio's franchise would cease on 30 March 2022 without extension, due to the company's failure to reach the required standards of customer service. There would be no further franchises, and control would pass to the Scottish government.

7
WIND FARMS

Although whisky distilling and then railways, brought about changes in the Moray landscape, these are as nothing compared with those which have come about through the construction of wind farms, which from 2004 onwards have continued to proliferate on an ever greater scale. Few would claim that wind turbines are beautiful objects in their own right, however Moray offers hills and high points over which strong winds blow, but which are not sufficiently strongly associated with Scotland's iconic mountain grandeur and associated tourist potential to have justified the exclusion of wind farms. There has been much debate about whether increasing demands for clean energy overrides possible damage to views and landscape, but this has effectively been answered in favour of the former by successive Scottish governments which, often in the face of strong opposition, both from local groups and local authorities, have given consent to several major schemes in Moray. This is with the aim of achieving a target of generating 50% of Scotland's overall energy consumption from renewable sources by 2030.

Although this is not the place to reopen the wider debate on whether the sacrifice of landscape values is a reasonable price to pay to combat climate change and generate sustainable energy supplies for future generations, the main arguments for them deserve to be stated.

Developers would argue that threat of climate change demands the delivery of clean, green, low-cost electricity as efficiently as possible and that onshore wind is one of the cheapest forms of electricity generation. In the short term, construction helps sustain the Moray economy, and in the longer term developers are obliged to make ongoing charitable contributions to be managed as local community benefit funds by the communities themselves. The manner in which these funds are managed and the frequency of distributions varies greatly from one developer to another.

In the name of this greater efficiency, monster turbines almost three times as tall as the Scott Monument in Edinburgh, and for obvious reasons regularly sited on high ground, have become an inescapable feature of views on most Moray long-distance walks. It is appropriate therefore to include here a section on how these wind farms have developed.

A so far little-discussed aspect of wind-farm development is that in order to construct and service them, hundreds of miles of roads in spidering networks have been made, penetrating deep into the Moray countryside. For walkers and cyclists who are not put off by the company of giant turbines beating the air around them, the Moray wind farm roads give splendid new opportunities for access to remote countryside. Also it may not be too long before the developing companies, emulating those in other countries, enhance their revenues by offering the paying public safari trips around their sites.

Rothes I and II (Fred Olsen Renewables)

Developed by Fred Olsen Renewables, this was Moray's first wind farm. Construction began in January 2004 and the wind farm started full operation in May 2005. It consists of 22 Siemens turbines, each rated at 2.3 megawatts (MW) giving a total installed capacity of 50.6MW. The rotor diameter is 82 metres (270 feet) and the height of the towers is 58.5m (192ft), giving a tip height of 100m (330ft). For comparison, the Scott Monument in Edinburgh is 60m (200ft) high. The wind farm is connected to the grid via 33kV underground cables to the Scottish and Southern Energy Moray substation.

The turbines are maintained under a contract with Siemens. As well as taking care of safety and energy production, an onsite team is responsible for monitoring the local ecology, including water tables, stream water quality and maintaining the natural plant and animal life in the area. Power is sold under long-term contracts with e-on UK. Rothes I is able to provide electricity equivalent to the consumption of 27,000 homes.

A recent development to the east of Rothes I, designated Rothes II, added a further 18 turbines. It started operation in 2013. For more information visit *www.fred-olsenrenewables.com*.

Paul's Hill (Fred Olsen Renewables)

Set up as a partnership between Fred Olsen Renewables and Ballindalloch Estate, the Paul's Hill wind farm came onstream in 2006. Sited on moorland at the northern edge of the estate, Paul's Hill consists of 28 Siemens 2.3MW turbines and can generate up to 64MW of electricity – enough for 35,000 homes.

Fred Olsen are developing plans for Paul's Hill II, a small extension of 6 turbines to the east of Paul's Hill I.

Berry Burn

The Berry Burn wind farm, operated by the Norwegian company Statkraft, is located 12–15km south of Forres. It has a total of 29 turbines and started operating in 2014. The installed capacity is 66.7MW, capable of powering up to 48,000 homes.

In December 2021, Statkraft received permission from the Energy Consent Unit, an agency of the Scottish Government, for an additional 9 turbines on this site, taking the total to 38 and adding a further 38MW to the capacity. The wind farm is on the slopes of *Cairn Ghiubhais* and *Carn Kitty*, on the Altyre Estate 1where its area is close to that of Paul's Hill. The entry point for the wind farm is NJ041466. The ruined craft of Berry Burn is located at NJ060454. Benefit to the local community is managed by a board of trustees with a rotating membership representing all the communities within the wind farm area. For more information visit *www.statkraft.co.uk*.

Hill of Glaschyle

This is a joint venture between Muirden Energy and the Logie Estate, and became operational in March 2017. It has 12 Enercon E70 turbines giving a total capacity of 27.6MW, enough to supply about 10,000 homes. The wind farm is sited on the southern side of the Hill of Glaschyle, about 10km south of Forres. It has a network of access tracks which the public are welcome to use for walking or cycling. The community fund is managed by the Finderne Development Trust (see p. 7).

Other projects submitted prior to 2022 and awaiting consent

Cairn Duhie (RES)

The proposed Cairn Duhie wind farm is located near the village of Ferness, 15km south-east of Nairn and 13.5km north-north-west of Grantown. This makes it clearly visible from many points in West Moray, including sections of the Dava Way. The site has no protection under national or international nature designations and is easily accessible from the A939.

The project, from RES Energy, received approval from the government's Energy Consent Unit in October 2017 despite local opposition. The original plan was for 20 turbines with tip heights of up to 110m (360ft) as well as the usual infrastructure of tracks, a mast, a control building and substation compound.

However, before construction started, revised plans were submitted to the Energy Consent Unit for a less obtrusive 16-turbine scheme using more efficient turbines. In early 2022, no decision had been announced. Progress is reported on *www.cairnduhie-windfarm.co.uk*.

Ourack (Vattenfall)

The Swedish energy company Vattenfall are developing the Ourack scheme, situated 6km north of Grantown and partly on the Via Regia (see p.164). The scheme would have 18 turbines, each producing up to 2.6MW of power and with a blade tip height of 180m. For more information visit *www.group.vattenfall.com*.

Clash Gour (EDF and Force 9)

The Clash Gour wind farm is being developed by Force 9 Energy in partnership with EDF Renewables. Force 9 is an independent UK-based renewable energy developer. If the project goes ahead, EDF would build, own and operate the wind farm. Because the proposed development would generate over 50MW, it is classed as a Section 36 scheme and needs approval from the Energy Consent Unit. The current proposal is for 48 turbines with a maximum tip height of 180m, on a site about 12km south of Forres. It would almost completely 'wrap round' the existing Berry Burn wind farm. A public inquiry into the scheme was held in summer 2020 but no decision had been announced by early 2022. For more information visit *www.edf-re.co.uk*.

Fred Olsen Renewables

Fred Olsen have proposals for two extensions: Rothes III, 29 turbines south of Rothes I and II, and Paul's Hill II, 6 additional turbines east of Paul's Hill I.

8
ESTATES AND LAND MANAGEMENT IN MORAY

The boundaries of the land called Moray have shifted greatly over the centuries, and the way in which land has been owned, bargained over and fought for throughout the centuries has been, and still is, in a state of constant flux. In historic times, feudal chieftains typically owned huge tracts of land, a prime example of which is the lands of Darnaway, the province of the Earls of Moray who ranked closest to royalty in the days of the Scottish kings from Robert the Bruce onwards. However, land ownership and tenure has changed dramatically in recent years. An Act of 2000 abolished feus, the old form of land tenure whereby the feu holder could charge tenants of the land substantial amounts of money annually.

This was followed by the 2003 Land Reform Act which gave rise to the 'right to roam'; since when community buyouts, windfarm developments and more have been made possible. Nevertheless there are still significantly large estates through which the Moray Way passes, in spite of the trend for land 'parcels' to become smaller as land ownership has become more egalitarian, and some farmers have found themselves able to purchase their holdings, thus becoming landowners rather than tenants.

It is not accidental that the land traversed by the Moray Way happens to be as it is; rather it is because it is managed in specific ways and for specific purposes, to which the alert walker or cyclist will be sensitive; they may well be interested in the ownership of the land on which they are setting foot or wheel. At some points the farmer on whose land the path lies is also the owner, at others the ultimate owner is more distant, either a local estate, or perhaps an even more distant landlord or Trust. In this short section the circuit described in sections 1 to

3 is retraced, this time with notes on the landowners and managers whose activities have a bearing on what is observed on the way. Details of many of the Moray estates can be found in the book *Who Owns Scotland* by Andy Wightman (Canongate, 1996) or on the related website *whoownsscotland.org.uk*.

Starting from Forres, as it was a Royal Burgh the land was traditionally owned by the king. Findhorn Bay to the north is now partly owned by the Ministry of Defence. The entire land on which Findhorn village now stands was, by a historical anomaly, part of Novar Estate Holdings. Around 1710 Hugh Rose, the owner of Kilravock Castle near Inverness, acquired the Findhorn lands from the local laird Sir James Calder in settlement of debts arising from trading disasters.

Some time later in the century these lands were sold on to Sir Hector Munro, who constructed the harbour, starting with the north pier in 1778. The south pier and an extension to the north pier followed in 1830, while the ownership of Findhorn land continued to be retained by the chiefs of Clan Munro, notwithstanding that their ancestral territories lay in Ross-shire on the other side of the Moray Firth.

Novar Estates continued to own the bulk of the Findhorn real estate until in 2015 the community-based Findhorn Village Conservation Company received a £520,000 grant from the Scottish Land Fund to enable it to acquire all the Novar Estate's holdings in Findhorn. The area concerned includes 61 hectares of amenity land at Findhorn and 800 hectares of coast next to the village. Among the Company's most recent developments is a serviced motorhome park where visitors are welcome to stay overnight for a modest charge.

The eastward boundary of Findhorn village is marked by a car park with concrete tank blocks nearby. From this point eastwards the land is owned by a charity, the Findhorn Development Trust, and managed by another charity, the Hinterland Development Trust which, on behalf of the Findhorn Foundation, also manages the territory on which the four turbines seen to the south lie. Next comes MoD property, immediately identifiable by the high fence on the landward side. Coastal erosion of the path is bringing this fence perilously close to the shore. From where Roseisle Forest begins Forestry and Land Scotland are in control until Burghead. The feus for this area were once held by the Young family who founded Hopeman in 1805, but the days of feudal superiorities ended when feu duty was finally abolished in the Act of 2000, and most home owners in the towns and villages have redeemed their feus. The immediate track out of Burghead adjoining the Maltings belongs to Diageo, beyond which the land is divided into relatively small parcels as far as the land belonging to West Sands caravan park at Hopeman.

Going east from Hopeman, the golf course and quarry company own their land, then to the east of these and extending beyond the Coastguard Lookout, the Hopeman Estate begins, where the owner Dean Anderson has done a great deal of recent work cutting back invading gorse to ensure that the path is comfortable and firmly based. The next pockets of land between here and Lossiemouth are under the ownership of the Covesea golf links, the Covesea Lighthouse Community Company (see p. 55), Silver Sands Caravan Park and the Moray Golf Club. The Moray Golf Club has owned the course since the land on which it lies was bought from the Pitgaveny estate in 1977.

After you leave Lossiemouth east beach, next comes Lossie Forest which is managed by the Crown Estate (which owns approximately 55% of the UK's foreshore), as well as Scottish Forestry, the Scottish Government agency responsible for forestry policy, support and regulations. Inland to the south of the forest lies the Innes estate, which also includes Bin Hill. A small estate called Corbiewell is located between the forest and further MoD territory which continues towards Kingston.

Next the Garmouth viaduct leads to the lands of the Gordon Lennox family, the hereditary owners of Gordon

Castle. South of Fochabers the Speyside Way passes into Crown Office lands, the bulk of which lie to the east of the Moray Way and where the Crown Estates are responsible for much of the forestry activity. The Crown Estate is the collection of lands and holdings within the United Kingdom belonging to the British monarch in his or her role as a corporation. It is 'the sovereign's public estate', which is neither government property nor part of the monarch's private estate. Crown Estates territory continues until Ordequish at NJ342573. From there to Arndilly and Craigellachie is the extensive Orton estate within which is the peak of Ben Aigan and the countryside around Rothes. Orton estate contains the highest and most remote part of the Moray Way where the route is largely through or around woodlands which are actively forested.

In feudal times, Aberlour and its surrounding area had the Earls of Fife as superior, however no one considerable estate dominates the stretch from Craigellachie southwards until Knockando, where the fishing beats of the Knockando estate are near Knockando and Tamdhu distilleries. The Knockando estate is the property of the Trustees of Catherine Wills, a scion of the well-known cigarette manufacturing dynasty. It has three and a half miles/6km of prime fishing rights on the Spey here, and in season you are likely to see rods on the river.

After the Knockando estate the next boundary is with the Ballindalloch estate at the point where the Cally Burn enters the Spey. Where the route leaves the riverside and crosses the A95, it passes through the the woods of Knockfink which belong to the Tulchan estate. The wood of Tom an Uird is privately owned by the firm of C.W. Lamley and Co. After leaving this north of Cromdale, the Speyside Way enters the Seafield estate which is headquartered at Cullen on the coast, where a considerable part of the Seafield holdings lie, although they also have major land holdings on Speyside from Ballindalloch to Aviemore.

Seafield territory prevails all the way through Grantown and northward up the Dava Way as far as Dava itself, where you pass into the territory of the Darnaway

Estate managed by the Moray Estates Development Company. An old boundary stone (quite hard to find off-track near an old quarry) has 'M' for Moray on one side and 'S' for Seafield on the reverse.

Just north of Auchenlochan at around NJ021418 lies the next boundary, beyond which is the Dunphail estate, one of three, the others being Genernie and Logie, which are owned by the Laing family, sons of the late Lord Laing, formerly Chairman of United Biscuits and Treasurer of the Conservative party from 1988 to 1993. At Bantrach Wood, the Glenernie estate lies to the west of the Dava Way, with Dunphail to the east.

After crossing the viaduct the Dava Way follows the Dunphail boundary with the estate now to the west, and continues to the Breathing Place at Waypoint 5 where the Logie estate takes over. The different characters of the Dunphail and Logie sections has already been commented on (see p. 146).

The final large estate to complete the circuit is Altyre, traditionally the seat of the Comyn family, later known as Cummings, and there have been Gordon-Cummings there from at least the seventeenth century.

Lastly, you come to the grounds of Dallas Dhu distillery which are in the care of Historic Environment Scotland, after which you arrive back in Forres.

Appendix

Grid references (prefix NJ) and approximate distances. Town/ village names are in bold. Distances are from one key point to the next.

		miles	km.
034592	**Forres**, Tolbooth	0.7	1.1
048596	**Forres**, Sueno's Stone	1.5	2.4
061614	Kinloss/Whiteinch road junction	2.6	4.2
037649	**Findhorn** dunes picnic area	4.5	7.2
104659	Roseisle : Forestry Commission car park	3.2	5.1
117690	**Burghead** maltings	2.2	3.5
146698	**Hopeman** recreation ground car park	2.6	4.2
176708	Coastguard Lookout	2.1	3.4
273683	Covesea Lighthouse	1.9	3.0
226709	**Lossiemouth**, west beach car park	1.0	1.6
238704	**Lossiemouth**, east beach footbridge	2.9	4.7
273683	WW II fortifications, west end of	3.5	5.6
321662	Former rifle range entrance	1.1	1.8
335656	**Kingston** car park (the Lein)	3.1	5.0
350642	**Garmouth** Speyside Way junction	3.0	4.8
344586	**Fochabers** centre	5.2	8.4
320517	Boat o' Brig	7.4	11.9
294452	**Craigellachie**, Bridge of Fiddich	2.6	4.2
265429	**Aberlour** station	3.4	5.5
221413	Dalmunach distillery	2.8	4.5
188418	Tamdhu distillery	2.4	3.9
183389	Blacksboat station	1.9	3.1
167366	Ballindalloch station	1.4	2.3
149364	End of railway track	1.1	1.8
148347	Achvorkie (join/leave A95)	0.7	1.1
143343	Airdbeg road end (join/leave A95)	4.5	7.2
108315	Minor road junction near Dalvey	2.5	4.0
084299	Pollowick road end	1.3	2.1
070286	**Cromdale** station	3.3	5.3
035275	**Grantown**, curling pond	1.0	1.6
025282	**Grantown**, Dulicht bridge	3.7	6.0

		miles	km.
023326	Huntly's Cave	3.1	5.0
019331	Dava summit	1.5	2.4
008388	Dava station (south end)	5.8	9.3
022464	Divie viaduct (south end)	1.3	2.1
015483	**Edinkillie** Hall (Breathing Place)	3.4	5.5
032523	Clashdhu road crossing	3.1	5.0
050559	Rafford bridge over minor road	1.7	2.7
036576	**Forres**, Mannachie Avenue	1.3	2.1
034592	**Forres**, Tolbooth		
	Total	**99.7**	**158.6**

INDEX